Newmark LEARNING

8

Common Core

Reading

Warm-Ups & Test Practice

Newmark Learning
145 Huguenot Street • New Rochelle, NY 10801

Editor: Ellen Ungaro
Designer: Raquel Hernández
Photo credits: Page 18: Courtesy of NOAA; Page 54: Courtesy of Library of Congress; Page 91: Courtesy of Gareth Wiscombe; Page 93: Manuel Cohen Photography/Manuel Cohen/Newscom

Table of Contents

Contents	Page
Introduction	4
Warm Up 1 Fiction: from *Heidi* RL.8.1, RL.8.2, RL.8.4	13
Warm Up 2 Science Text: Weather Patterns RI.8.1, RI.8.2, RI.8.4	18
Warm Up 3 Realistic Fiction: The Tryout RL.8.1, RL.8.2, RL.8.3, RL.8.4	23
Warm Up 4 Social Studies Text: The Bone Wars RI.8.2, RI.8.3, RI.8.5	28
Warm Up 5 Realistic Fiction: An Unexpected Treasure RL.8.1, RL.8.3, RL.8.4	33
Warm Up 6 Informational Text: What Is Short-Term Stress? RI.8.3, RI.8.4, RI.8.6	37
Warm Up 7 Fiction: from Chapter 3 of *The Adventures of Tom Sawyer* RL.8.1, RL.8.3, RL.8.4	41
Warm Up 8 Science Text: The Storytelling Canyon RI.8.1, RI.8.2, RI.8.3, RI.8.7	45
Warm Up 9 Science Fiction: Alien Encounter RL.8.1, RL.8.3, RL.8.4, RL.8.6	50
Warm Up 10 Social Studies Text: Endurance RI.8.1, RI.8.2, RI.8.4, RI.8.8	54
Practice Test 1 Fiction: from *An Autumn Flood* RL.8.1, RL.8.2, RL.8.3, RL.8.4, RL.8.6	59
Practice Test 2 Social Studies Text: Australia's Rock Art RI.8.1, RI.8.2, RI.8.3, RI.8.4, RI.8.5, RI.8.6, RI.8.8	69
Practice Test 3 Historical Fiction: The Blacksmith's Helper Legend: How Moccasins Were Made RL.8.1, RL.8.2, RL.8.3, RL.8.4, RL.8.5, RL.8.6	79
Practice Test 4 Social Studies Text: Constructing a Monument: Stonehenge Social Studies Text: Sister of Stonehenge RI.8.1, RI.8.2, RI.8.3, RI.8.4, RI.8.5, RI.8.6, RI.8.9	91
Answer Key	103

Introduction

What are the new Common Core assessments?

The Common Core State Standards for English Language Arts have set shared, consistent, and clear objectives of what students are expected to learn. The standards are intended to be rigorous and reflect what students will need to be able to do to be college and career ready by the end of high school.

As a part of this initiative, two consortia of states, the Partnership for Assessment of Readiness for College and Careers (PARCC) and Smarter Balanced, have developed new assessments that are aligned with the Common Core State Standards and designed to measure students' progress toward college and career readiness.

How are the new assessments different?

The new standardized assessments from both PARCC and Smarter Balanced are designed to be taken online and include many new types of assessment items.

In addition to multiple-choice questions, the assessments include both short and extended constructed-response questions, which require students to develop written responses that include examples and details from the text.

Another key element in the PARCC and Smarter Balanced assessments is the two-part question. In two-part questions, Part B asks students to identify the text evidence that supports their answer to Part A. These questions reflect the new emphasis on text evidence in the Common Core Standards. Anchor Standard 1 states that students should "cite specific textual evidence when writing or speaking to support conclusions drawn from the text."

The assessments from PARCC and Smarter Balanced also include technology-enhanced questions. These items, which students will encounter if they take the online assessments, ask students to interact with and manipulate text. For example, some questions ask students to select two or three correct answers from a list. Other questions ask students to identify important events in a story and then arrange them in the correct order.

The assessments from PARCC and Smarter Balanced will also feature passages that meet the requirements for complex texts set by the Common Core State Standards. The ability to read and comprehend complex text is another key element of the new standards. Anchor Standard 10 for reading states that students should be able to "Read and comprehend complex literary and informational texts independently and proficiently."

Common Core Reading Warm-Ups & Test Practice is designed to help prepare students for these new assessments from PARCC and Smarter Balanced. The Warm Ups and Practice Tests will help students rehearse the kind of thinking needed for success on the online assessments.

What Test Will Your State Take?

Smarter Balanced States	PARCC States
Alaska	Arizona
California	Arkansas
Connecticut	Colorado
Delaware	District of Columbia
Hawaii	Florida
Idaho	Georgia
Iowa	Illinois
Kansas	Indiana
Maine	Kentucky
Michigan	Louisiana
Missouri	Maryland
Montana	Massachusetts
Nevada	Mississippi
New Hampshire	New Jersey
North Carolina	New Mexico
North Dakota	New York
Oregon	North Dakota
Pennsylvania	Ohio
South Carolina	Oklahoma
South Dakota	Pennsylvania
U.S. Virgin Islands	Rhode Island
Vermont	Tennessee
Washington	
West Virginia	
Wisconsin	
Wyoming	

How will this book help my students prepare for the new assessments?

Warm Ups for Guided Practice

Common Core Reading Warm-Ups and Test Practice include 10 Warm Up tests that are designed to provide students with an opportunity for quick, guided practice.

The 10 Warm Ups feature short reading passages that include examples of the genres that students are required to read and will encounter on the test. In grade 8, the Common Core State Standards require students to read stories, drama, poetry, social studies, science, and technical texts.

Realistic Fiction

Poetry

Science Text

Social Studies Text

Common Core Reading Warm-Ups & Test Practice Grade 8

©2014 Newmark Learning, LLC

The questions that follow the Warm Ups include the variety of formats and question types that students will encounter on the new assessments. They include two-part questions, constructed response (short answer) questions, and questions that replicate the technology-enhanced items.

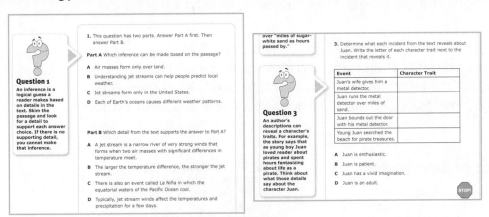

Question 1
An inference is a logical guess a reader makes based on details in the text. Skim the passage and look for a detail to support each answer choice. If there is no supporting detail, you cannot make that inference.

1. This question has two parts. Answer Part A first. Then answer Part B.

Part A Which inference can be made based on the passage?

A Air masses form only over land.

B Understanding jet streams can help people predict local weather.

C Jet streams form only in the United States.

D Each of Earth's oceans causes different weather patterns.

Part B Which detail from the text supports the answer to Part A?

A A jet stream is a narrow river of very strong winds that forms when two air masses with significant differences in temperature meet.

B The larger the temperature difference, the stronger the jet stream.

C There is also an event called La Niña in which the equatorial waters of the Pacific Ocean cool.

D Typically, jet stream winds affect the temperatures and precipitation for a few days.

over "miles of sugar-white sand as hours passed by."

Question 3
An author's descriptions can reveal a character's traits. For example, the story says that as young boy Juan loved reader about pirates and spent hours fantasizing about life as a pirate. Think about what those details say about the character Juan.

3. Determine what each incident from the text reveals about Juan. Write the letter of each character trait next to the incident that reveals it.

Event	Character Trait
Juan's wife gives him a metal detector.	
Juan runs the metal detector over miles of sand.	
Juan bounds out the door with his metal detector.	
Young Juan searched the beach for pirate treasures.	

A Juan is enthusiastic.

B Juan is patient.

C Juan has a vivid imagination.

D Juan is an adult.

STOP

The Warm Ups also include prompts with each question. These prompts provide students with tips and strategies for answering the questions.

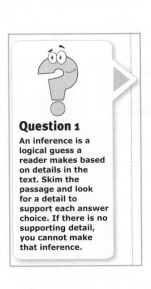

Question 1

An inference is a logical guess a reader makes based on details in the text. Skim the passage and look for a detail to support each answer choice. If there is no supporting detail, you cannot make that inference.

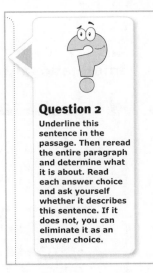

Question 2

Underline this sentence in the passage. Then reread the entire paragraph and determine what it is about. Read each answer choice and ask yourself whether it describes this sentence. If it does not, you can eliminate it as an answer choice.

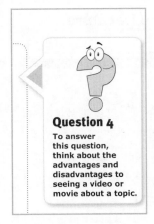

Question 4

To answer this question, think about the advantages and disadvantages to seeing a video or movie about a topic.

Practice Tests to Build Test-Taking Stamina

The Practice Tests feature longer passages that match the passage lengths that will be used for the PARCC and Smarter Balanced tests. These passages provide students with experience reading the longer and more complex texts they will have to read on the new assessments.

Two of the Practice Tests also feature paired passages. The paired passages give students the opportunity to compare and contrast texts and integrate information from multiple texts, as required by Standard R.9. Practice Tests include both literature and informational texts.

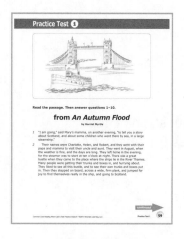

Literature

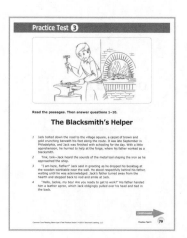

Informational Texts

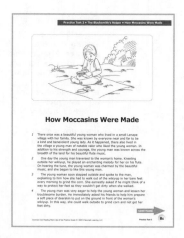

Paired Texts

Each passage is followed by a complete set of questions that reflects the number of questions students will find with each passage on the new assessments. In addition, similar to the Warm Ups, the Practice Tests also include the types of questions students will encounter. Every Practice Test also includes three constructed response (short answer) questions to give students practice writing about texts and using details from the text in their response.

---

1. This question has two parts. Answer Part A first. Then answer Part B.

Part A Which of the following statements about Charlotte, Helen, and Robert is true?

A Traveling by sea is their favorite thing to do.

B This is their first trip on a large steamship.

C They would rather play than spend time with their parents.

D They have never been to Scotland before.

Part B Which sentence from the passage supports the answer to Part A?

A They were surprised to see what a length it was.

B All the morning they had plenty to look at.

C They never knew when the steamer began to go fast down the river towards the sea.

D They liked to see all this bustle, and to see their own trunks and boxes put in.

Two-part questions

---

7. Read the list of details below. Check the box next to each detail that accurately describes a feature of Aboriginal rock art.

- ☐ simple stick figures
- ☐ found all over the world
- ☐ stenciled hand outlines
- ☐ elaborate drawings of animals
- ☐ under threat by vandals
- ☐ consists of paintings and engravings found in rock
- ☐ created several hundred years ago
- ☐ stick figures were created using a lump of ochre.
- ☐ brushes were made from animal hides.

Questions with multiple answers

---

8. According to "Sister of Stonehenge," why is Woodhenge called the "wooden twin" of Stonehenge? Use details from the passage to support your answer.

_____
_____
_____
_____
_____
_____
_____
_____

9. According to "Constructing a Monument: Stonehenge," how do scientists identify the different building phases of the monument? Use details from the passage to support your answer.

_____
_____
_____
_____
_____
_____

10. Do the authors of the passages agree on Stonehenge's uniqueness? Use details from both passages to support your answer.

_____
_____
_____
_____
_____
_____
_____
_____
_____
_____
_____
_____
_____
_____
_____
_____
_____

Constructed-response questions

Correlated to the Common Core State Standards

All of the assessment items are correlated to the Reading Standards for Literature or the Reading Standards for Informational Text. The chart below shows the standards that each Warm Up and Practice Test addresses.

TEST	RL/RI 8.1	RL/RI 8.2	RL/RI 8.3	RL/RI 8.4	RL/RI 8.5	RL/RI 8.6	RL/RI 8.7	RI 8.8	RL/RI 8.9
Warm Up 1	X	X		X					
Warm Up 2	X	X		X					
Warm Up 3	X	X	X	X					
Warm Up 4		X	X		X				
Warm Up 5	X		X	X					
Warm Up 6			X	X		X			
Warm Up 7	X		X	X					
Warm Up 8	X	X	X				X		
Warm Up 9	X		X	X		X			
Warm Up 10	X	X		X				X	
Practice Test 1	X	X	X	X		X			
Practice Test 2	X	X	X	X	X	X		X	
Practice Test 3	X	X	X	X	X	X			
Practice Test 4	X	X	X	X	X	X			X

Grade 8 Common Core State Standards

Reading Standards for Literature

RL.8.1 Cite the textual evidence that most strongly supports an analysis of what the text says explicitly as well as inferences drawn from the text.
RL.8.2 Determine a theme or central idea of a text and analyze its development over the course of the text, including its relationship to the characters, setting, and plot; provide an objective summary of the text.
RL.8.3 Analyze how particular lines of dialogue or incidents in a story or drama propel the action, reveal aspects of a character, or provoke a decision.
RL.8.4 Determine the meaning of words and phrases as they are used in a text, including figurative and connotative meanings; analyze the impact of specific word choices on meaning and tone, including analogies or allusions to other texts.
RL.8.5 Compare and contrast the structure of two or more texts and analyze how the differing structure of each text contributes to its meaning and style.
RL.8.6 Analyze how differences in the points of view of the characters and the audience or reader (e.g., created through the use of dramatic irony) create such effects as suspense or humor.
RL.8.7 Analyze the extent to which a filmed or live production of a story or drama stays faithful to or departs from the text or script, evaluating the choices made by the director or actors.
RL.8.9 Analyze how a modern work of fiction draws on themes, patterns of events, or character types from myths, traditional stories, or religious works such as the Bible, including describing how the material is rendered new.

Reading Standards for Informational Texts

RI.8.1 Cite the textual evidence that most strongly supports an analysis of what the text says explicitly as well as inferences drawn from the text.
RI.8.2 Determine a central idea of a text and analyze its development over the course of the text, including its relationship to supporting ideas; provide an objective summary of the text.
RI.8.3 Analyze how a text makes connections among and distinctions between individuals, ideas, or events (e.g., through comparisons, analogies, or categories).
RI.8.4 Determine the meaning of words and phrases as they are used in a text, including figurative, connotative, and technical meanings; analyze the impact of specific word choices on meaning and tone, including analogies or allusions to other texts.
RI.8.5 Analyze in detail the structure of a specific paragraph in a text, including the role of particular sentences in developing and refining a key concept.
RI.8.6 Determine an author's point of view or purpose in a text and analyze how the author acknowledges and responds to conflicting evidence or viewpoints.
RI.8.7 Evaluate the advantages and disadvantages of using different mediums (e.g., print or digital text, video, multimedia) to present a particular topic or idea.
RI.8.8 Delineate and evaluate the argument and specific claims in a text, assessing whether the reasoning is sound and the evidence is relevant and sufficient; recognize when irrelevant evidence is introduced.
RI.8.9 Analyze a case in which two or more texts provide conflicting information on the same topic and identify where the texts disagree on matters of fact or interpretation.

How to Use *Common Core Reading Warm-Ups and Test Practice*

The Warm Ups are designed to be quick and easy practice for students. They can be used in a variety of ways:

- Assign Warm Ups for homework.

- Use them for quick review in class.

- Use them for targeted review of key standards. The correlation chart on page 10 can help identify Warm Ups that address the skills you want to focus on.

The longer Practice Tests can be used to prepare students in the weeks before the assessments. They can also be used to help assess students' reading comprehension throughout the year.

Tear-out Answer Keys

Find the answers to all the Warm Ups and Practice Tests in the Answer Key. The Answer Key includes the standards correlations for each question. In addition, it includes sample answers for the constructed response (short answer) questions.

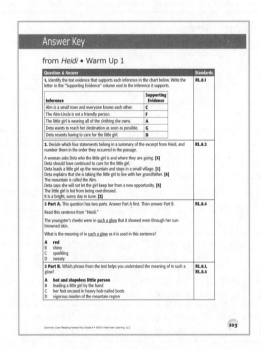

RL.8.1
Cite the textual evidence that most strongly supports an analysis of what the text says explicitly as well as inferences drawn from the text.

RL.8.2
Determine a theme or central idea of a text and analyze its development over the course of the text, including its relationship to the characters, setting, and plot; provide an objective summary of the text.

RL.8.4
Determine the meaning of words and phrases as they are used in a text, including figurative and connotative meanings; analyze the impact of specific word choices on meaning and tone, including analogies or allusions to other texts.

Read this passage and then answer the questions that follow.

from *Heidi*

Johanna Spyri

1   One bright sunny morning in June, a tall, vigorous maiden of the mountain region climbed up the narrow path, leading a little girl by the hand. The youngster's cheeks were in such a glow that it showed even through her sun-browned skin. Small wonder though! for in spite of the heat, the little one, who was scarcely five years old, was bundled up as if she had to brave a bitter frost. Her shape was difficult to distinguish, for she wore two dresses, if not three, and around her shoulders a large red cotton shawl. With her feet encased in heavy hob-nailed boots, this hot and shapeless little person toiled up the mountain.

continued ➤

2   The pair had been climbing for about an hour when they reached a hamlet half-way up the great mountain named the Alm. It was the elder girl's home town, and therefore she was greeted from nearly every house; people called to her from windows and doors, and very often from the road. But, answering questions and calls as she went by, the girl did not loiter on her way and only stood still when she reached the end of the hamlet. There a few cottages lay scattered about, from the furthest of which a voice called out to her through an open door:

3   A stout, pleasant-looking woman stepped out of the house and joined the two.

4   "Where are you taking the child, Deta?" asked the newcomer. "Is she the child your sister left?"

5   "Yes," Deta assured her; "I am taking her up to the Alm-Uncle and there I want her to remain."

6   "You can't really mean to take her there, Deta. You must have lost your senses, to go to him. I am sure the old man will show you the door and won't even listen to what you say."

7   "Why not? As he's her grandfather, it is high time he should do something for the child. I have taken care of her until this summer and now a good place has been offered to me. The child shall not hinder me from accepting it, I tell you that!"

Name_____ Date_____

1. Identify the text evidence that supports each inference in the chart below. Write the letter in the "Supporting Evidence" column next to the inference it supports.

Inference	Supporting Evidence
Alm is a small town and everyone knows each other.	
The Alm-Uncle is not a friendly person.	
The little girl is wearing all of the clothing she owns.	
Deta wants to reach her destination as soon as possible.	
Deta resents having to care for the little girl.	

Question 1

An inference is a logical guess readers can make based on details in the text. Read each piece of supporting evidence and ask yourself what you can infer from it. Then look for your inference in the list.

A Her shape was difficult to distinguish, for she wore two dresses, if not three, and around her shoulders a large red cotton shawl.

B One bright sunny morning in June, a tall, vigorous maiden of the mountain region climbed up the narrow path, leading a little girl by the hand.

C It was the elder girl's home town, and therefore she was greeted from nearly every house; people called to her from windows and doors, and very often from the road.

D "This child shall not hinder me from accepting it, I tell you that!"

E The pair had been climbing for about an hour when they reached a hamlet half-way up the great mountain named the Alm.

F "I am sure the old man will show you the door and won't even listen to what you say."

G But, answering questions and calls as she went by, the girl did not loiter on her way and only stood still when she reached the end of the hamlet.

continued

Name_____ Date_____

Question 2

A summary should be objective and include only the most important points. Read through the statements and cross out those that are minor details or personal opinions. Then number the remaining statements in the order in which they happened.

2. Decide which four statements belong in a summary of the excerpt from _Heidi_, and number them in the order they occurred in the passage.

— A woman asks Deta who the little girl is and where they are going.

— Deta should have continued to care for the little girl.

— Deta leads a little girl up the mountain and stops in a small village.

— Deta explains that she is taking the little girl to live with her grandfather.

— The mountain is called the Alm.

— Deta says she will not let the girl keep her from a new opportunity.

— The little girl is hot from being overdressed.

— It is a bright, sunny day in June.

Name_____ Date_____

3. This question has two parts. Answer Part A first. Then answer Part B.

Part A Read this sentence from the excerpt from _Heidi_.

> The youngster's cheeks were <u>in such a glow</u> that it showed even through her sun-browned skin.

What is the meaning of <u>in such a glow</u> as it is used in this sentence?

A red

B shiny

C sparkling

D sweaty

Part B Which phrase from the text helps you understand the meaning of <u>in such a glow</u>?

A hot and shapeless little person

B leading a little girl by the hand

C her feet encased in heavy hob-nailed boots

D vigorous maiden of the mountain region

Question 3

Context clues can help readers determine the meanings of words and phrases. Reread paragraph 1 and think about what is happening in the story. It is a hot day and the little girl is climbing up a mountain. She is wearing many layers of clothing. These clues can help you determine the meaning of the phrase.

STOP!

Common Core ELA STANDARDS

RI.8.1
Cite the textual evidence that most strongly supports an analysis of what the text says explicitly as well as inferences drawn from the text.

RI.8.2
Determine a central idea of a text and analyze its development over the course of the text, including its relationship to supporting ideas; provide an objective summary of the text.

RI.8.4
Determine the meaning of words and phrases as they are used in a text, including figurative, connotative, and technical meanings; analyze the impact of specific word choices on meaning and tone, including analogies or allusions to other texts.

Read this passage and then answer the questions that follow.

Weather Patterns

from NOAA's Weather and Atmosphere website

1   While a heat wave or a rainy week may cause discomfort for most of us, to a meteorologist they are fascinating examples of weather patterns, or repeating weather. Air masses affect the local weather on a daily and weekly basis. Jet streams carry the air from these masses to different parts of the country.

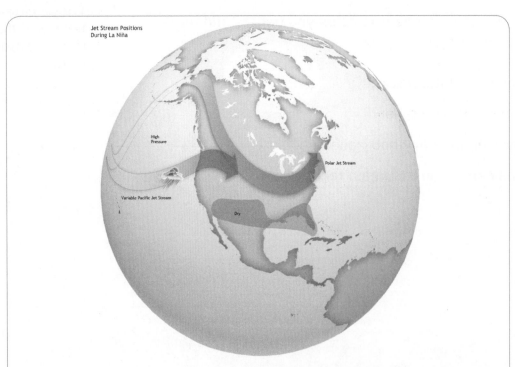

This diagram shows the paths of the jet streams during La Niña.

2   A jet stream is a narrow river of very strong winds that forms when two air masses with significant differences in temperature meet. The larger the temperature difference, the stronger the jet stream. A jet stream flows along the upper boundaries of these air masses and usually moves from west to east in a generally straight direction. Typically, jet stream winds affect the temperatures and precipitation for a few days. However, in some circumstances, the temperature difference in the air masses is less extreme, causing the jet stream to become sluggish and meander more north and south, forming a longer-term weather pattern. One example of this occurred in 2011, when Wichita Falls, Texas, had fifty-two consecutive days above 100°F.

3   Every three to seven years, the Earth has a weather pattern known as "El Niño." El Niño is the warming of the equatorial waters of the Pacific Ocean caused by a stronger, more southerly flowing jet stream. As a result, in the United States, the south experiences a wetter winter. Meanwhile, the west is stormier and the north is warmer. There is also an event called "La Niña" in which the equatorial waters of the Pacific Ocean cool. During La Niña, the jet stream shifts north, creating snowy winters and hot, dry summers in the north.

4   So the next time you are upset about the weather, take consolation in thinking like a meteorologist. See if you can identify a pattern that may be forming.

continued

Name_____ Date_____

Question 1

An inference is a logical guess a reader makes based on details in the text. Skim the passage and look for a detail to support each answer choice. If there is no supporting detail, you cannot make that inference.

1. This question has two parts. Answer Part A first. Then answer Part B.

Part A Which inference can be made based on the passage?

A Air masses form only over land.

B Understanding jet streams can help people predict local weather.

C Jet streams form only in the United States.

D Each of Earth's oceans causes different weather patterns.

Part B Which detail from the text supports the answer to Part A?

A A jet stream is a narrow river of very strong winds that forms when two air masses with significant differences in temperature meet.

B The larger the temperature difference, the stronger the jet stream.

C There is also an event called La Niña in which the equatorial waters of the Pacific Ocean cool.

D Typically, jet stream winds affect the temperatures and precipitation for a few days.

Name_____ Date_____

2. Summarize "Weather Patterns." Choose five statements that belong in a summary of this passage and number them in the order they occur in the passage.

— Everyone should learn how air masses affect weather.

— Jet streams affect the weather in a particular area.

— Air masses are carried around the country by jet streams.

— In 2011, it was above 100°F for fifty-two days in a row in Wichita Falls, Texas.

— Warming and cooling water temperatures in the Pacific Ocean cause some weather patterns.

— Jet streams are strong winds caused by temperature differences between air masses.

— Extreme temperature and precipitation are examples of weather patterns.

— Small temperature differences between air masses lead to longer weather patterns.

Question 2

A summary tells the most important parts of a text. It leaves out minor details and personal opinions. Cross out any of the statements on this list that are details or opinions. Then decide the sequence of the remaining items.

continued

Name_____ Date_____

Question 3

Reread the paragraph on El Niño and La Niña. As you read each fact about El Niño or La Niña, look for it in the list of answer choices. If you find it in the list, place a check by it and write the letter in the appropriate column.

3. Read each description and decide whether it applies to El Niño or La Niña. Write the letter in the correct column.

El Niño	La Niña

A caused by warming Pacific Ocean waters

B results in wetter winters in the southern United States

C results in snowy winters in the northern United States

D the jet stream flows more southerly

E the jet stream flows more northerly

F causes more winter storms in the western United States

G causes hot, dry summers in the northern United States

H results in warmer winters in the northern United States

Common Core ELA STANDARDS

RL.8.1
Cite the textual evidence that most strongly supports an analysis of what the text says explicitly as well as inferences drawn from the text.

RL.8.2
Determine a theme or central idea of a text and analyze its development over the course of the text, including its relationship to the characters, setting, and plot; provide an objective summary of the text.

RL.8.3
Analyze how particular lines of dialogue or incidents in a story or drama propel the action, reveal aspects of a character, or provoke a decision.

RL.8.4
Determine the meaning of words and phrases as they are used in a text, including figurative and connotative meanings; analyze the impact of specific word choices on meaning and tone, including analogies or allusions to other texts.

Read this passage and then answer the questions that follow.

The Tryout

1   Kai tossed his books on the table and opened the refrigerator. He funneled carrots, strawberries, an orange, and a huge bunch of spinach into the blender and pressed the button, stopping the machine briefly to throw in a scoop of walnuts— can't forget the protein. He briefly wondered if it would all taste good together before taking a huge gulp, but it didn't matter: all athletes get in shape by drinking smoothies.

2   In the backyard, Kai relentlessly threw the baseball at a net that was designed to return the ball to him. He was working to get his throwing arm in good shape, along with the rest of him. Kai didn't know much about baseball, since he had never played before; all he knew was that tryouts for the school team were on Saturday, and he would be primed and ready. His parents had always encouraged him to succeed at academics in school, but this was something Kai wanted to do for himself.

continued

3   Next, he ran wind sprints across the lawn, crouching down and hustling back and forth, back and forth, from fence to fence, until he was panting hard and down on one knee. Then he did sit-ups—grueling, punishing crunches—and he grimaced with each one, all seventy-five of them. Later, Kai planned to ask his father to take him to the batting cages; he knew that hitting was his weakness, so he needed all the practice he could get. Kai was aware that earning a spot on the team wasn't going to be a cakewalk, but he was determined to immerse himself in the effort and give it his all. The other players would have experience, speed, agility, and strength; but what Kai lacked in skill, he would make up for in gumption.

Name_____ Date_____

1. This question has two parts. Answer Part A first. Then answer Part B.

Part A Read this sentence from "The Tryout."

> Kai was aware that earning a spot on the team <u>wasn't going to be a cakewalk</u>, but he was determined to immerse himself in the effort and give it his all.

What does the phrase <u>wasn't going to be a cakewalk</u> mean?

A would not be fun

B would not be easy

C would not include sweets

D would not allow him to walk

Part B Which phrase helps you understand the meaning of <u>wasn't going to be a cakewalk</u>?

A planned to ask his father

B what Kai lacked in skill

C so he needed all the practice he could get.

D hitting was his weakness

Question 1

The phrase "it wasn't going to be a cakewalk" is an idiom. You can't figure out the meaning by looking at the individual words. You need to look at context clues. Reread the passage and look for details that tell you what Kai does to earn a spot on the team.

continued

Name_____ Date_____

Question 2

Reread paragraph 2 and look for details that explain why Kai is throwing the baseball at the net. Then reread the answer choices and decide which ones you can eliminate.

2. Read this sentence from "The Tryout."

> Kai relentlessly threw the baseball at a net that was designed to return the ball to him.

What does this sentence tell readers about Kai?

A Kai is able to throw the baseball at high speeds.

B Kai does not understand the rules of baseball.

C Kai is willing to spend a lot of time working toward his goal.

D Kai does not have enough energy to find his ball after he throws it.

Name_____ Date_____

3. This question has two parts. Answer Part A first. Then answer Part B.

Part A What is the central idea of this passage?

A It takes hard work and dedication to try out for a team.

B Only people with experience will make the team.

C Eating a healthy diet is the most important part of getting in shape.

D Participating in sports is more important than academic success.

Question 3

The central idea is what the text is mostly about. Read each answer choice and ask yourself if it describes what the story is mostly about. If it does not, you can eliminate it as an answer choice.

Part B Which detail from the text best supports the answer to Part A?

A All athletes get in shape by drinking smoothies.

B His parents had always encouraged him to succeed at academics in school.

C The other players would have experience, speed, agility, and strength.

D He was determined to immerse himself in the effort and give it his all.

STOP!

Common Core ELA STANDARDS

RI.8.2
Determine a central idea of a text and analyze its development over the course of the text, including its relationship to supporting ideas; provide an objective summary of the text.

RI.8.3
Analyze how a text makes connections among and distinctions between individuals, ideas, or events (e.g., through comparisons, analogies, or categories).

RI.8.5
Analyze in detail the structure of a specific paragraph in a text, including the role of particular sentences in developing and refining a key concept.

Read this passage and then answer the questions that follow.

The Bone Wars

1 One of the longest and most bitter rivalries in nineteenth-century America was not over gold, timber, or coal— but over dinosaur bones. Known as the Bone Wars, this fierce competition between two of the country's leading paleontologists not only caused each man to abhor the other, it also damaged the professional reputations of the two men.

2 In their quest to become known as the best of the dinosaur hunters, Othniel Charles Marsh and Edward Drinker Cope helped to discover over 1,500 different types of fossils. For over twenty years, the two men engaged in a competition that was as bitter as it was fierce.

Edward Drinker Cope

Othniel Charles Marsh

Common Core Reading Warm-Ups & Test Practice Grade 8 • ©2014 Newmark Learning, LLC

3   For both Othniel Charles March and Edward Drinker Cope, there were no measures too extreme or too outrageous in the race to become the reigning dinosaur hunter. They spied on each other's excavations. They bribed and bullied colleagues and workers. They even had their workers deliberately destroy fossils so the other man could not collect them. The contest between the two climaxed in 1877, with the discovery of fossils at two separate sites in Colorado. One site belonged to Marsh, the other to Cope. To Cope's dismay, the area that belonged to Marsh would eventually uncover the first known remains of the dinosaurs *Stegosaurus* and *Brontosaurus*.

4   By 1892, the Bone Wars had come to an end. Their work had left both men almost penniless. However, the efforts of Cope and Marsh paid off handsomely in other ways; it is believed that over 142 new species were discovered as a result of their work. It would appear that Marsh won the Bone Wars, with his discovery of some eighty new dinosaur fossils.

5   Although the relationship between Marsh and Cope was forever tainted, the findings by both men galvanized the American public's growing interest in dinosaurs, a fascination that continues to resonate over a century later.

continued

Name_____ Date_____

Question 1

A central idea is what a text is mostly about. Read each answer choice and determine where it is mentioned in the passage. If it is mentioned two or more times, it is likely a central idea.

1. This question has two parts. Answer Part A first. Then answer Part B.

Part A Which statement is a central idea of "The Bone Wars"?

A Competition leads to handsome rewards.

B Scientific rivals will stop at nothing to win.

C The rivalry of the scientists had both positive and negative results.

D Colorado holds the most important dinosaur fossils found.

B. Which of the following details from the text support your answer to Part B? Check the box next to each statement you choose.

☐ Their work had left both men almost penniless.

☐ The contest between the two climaxed in 1877, with the discovery of fossils at two separate sites in Colorado.

☐ It would appear that Marsh won the Bone Wars, with his discovery of some eighty new dinosaur fossils.

☐ By 1892, the Bone Wars had come to an end.

☐ It is believed that over 142 new species were discovered as a result of their work.

☐ Although the relationship between Marsh and Cope was forever tainted, the findings by both men galvanized the American public's growing interest in dinosaurs.

Name_____ Date_____

2. Read this sentence from "The Bone Wars."

> For both men, there were no measures too extreme or too outrageous in the race to become the reigning dinosaur hunter.

How does this sentence help develop a key concept of the text?

A It summarizes the creative ideas the men had as they hunted fossils.

B It introduces the idea that the men did many awful things in an effort to win.

C It provides a detailed description of specific behaviors the men engaged in.

D It supports the idea that winning is more important than gaining scientific knowledge.

Question 2

Underline this sentence in the passage. Then reread the entire paragraph and determine what it is about. Read each answer choice and ask yourself whether it describes this sentence. If it does not, you can eliminate it as an answer choice.

continued

Name_____ Date_____

Question 3

Read the passage again carefully. When the author makes a statement that applies to both Marsh and Cope, look for it on the list of answer choices. If you find it, check the box next to the statement.

3. Determine which comparisons the author provides to show how Cope and Marsh are similar. Check the box next to each statement you choose.

❑ Both spied on the other's dig sites.

❑ Both saved their reputations by discovering so many new species.

❑ Both despised the other.

❑ Both discovered the *Stegosaurus* and *Brontosaurus*.

❑ Both wanted the title of "Best Dinosaur Hunter."

❑ Both had their workers destroy fossils so the other could not find them.

❑ Both fought over gold.

❑ Both lost all of their money by the end of the Bone Wars.

❑ Both bribed workers.

Common Core ELA STANDARDS

RL.8.1
Cite the textual evidence that most strongly supports an analysis of what the text says explicitly as well as inferences drawn from the text.

RL.8.3
Analyze how particular lines of dialogue or incidents in a story or drama propel the action, reveal aspects of a character, or provoke a decision.

RL.8.4
Determine the meaning of words and phrases as they are used in a text, including figurative and connotative meanings; analyze the impact of specific word choices on meaning and tone, including analogies or allusions to other texts.

Read this passage and then answer the questions that follow.

An Unexpected Treasure

1   As a little boy, Juan had spent many a night poring over books in his bed; he loved stories about buccaneers, brawls at sea, and full-sailed frigates cutting through endless ocean waters. When he wasn't fantasizing about life as a pirate, Juan was scouring the beaches of Mexico in hopes of finding buried treasure. As the years marched on, Juan became taller and wiser, yet he never outgrew his obsession. One sunny day, his wife presented him with a state-of-the-art metal detector and smiled broadly as Juan excitedly bounded out the door with it.

continued

2   Juan strolled along the beach, running the end of his device over miles of sugar-white sand as hours passed by and the sun began its descent into the sea. Juan's stomach was grumbling, and he thought it was probably time to call it a day. Suddenly, he heard a beep. He flinched at the noise; he hadn't heard so much as a blip in all his hours combing the beach. With fingers trembling, Juan ran the disk of his metal detector back over the spot, straining his ears to hear the digital alarm sound out again. What a melodious tune it was: beep, beep, beep.

3   Juan gave out a cry and picked up his shovel. He began to dig with a fervor he had never felt before. Before long, a small crowd formed around the perimeter of the growing hole, and people began to join in, using shovels or their bare hands. Juan dug and dug, his mind whirring with possibilities. Had he stumbled across a treasure chest filled with gold doubloons that had been buried centuries ago?

4   Juan's shovel struck something hard and unmoving. His eyes grew wide, he held his breath, and he scraped his hand across a thin metal placard that read: 093-BFX.

Name_____ Date_____

1. This question has two parts. Answer Part A first. Then answer Part B.

Part A Which of the following inferences can you make from the passage?

A Juan found a license plate.

B Juan wishes he was a pirate.

C Juan is frustrated with the hunt along the beach.

D Juan learns how to work the metal detector at the end of the day.

Part B Which detail from the text supports the answer to Part A?

A Juan's stomach was rumbling, and he thought it was probably time to call it a day.

B Juan dug and dug, his mind whirring with possibilities.

C His eyes grew wide, he held his breath, and he scraped his hand across a thin metal placard that read: 093-BFX.

D With fingers trembling, Juan ran the disk of his metal detector back over the spot, straining his ears to hear the digital alarm sound out again.

Question 1
An inference must be made from evidence in a text. Skim the passage, looking for evidence to support each answer choice. If you cannot find evidence, you can eliminate the answer choice.

continued ➡

Name_____ Date_____

Question 2

Reread paragraph 2 to look for context clues that will help you understand the meaning of the phrase. For example, the passage describes Juan going over "miles of sugar-white sand as hours passed by."

2. Read this sentence from "An Unexpected Treasure."

> He flinched at the noise; he hadn't heard so much as a blip in all his hours <u>combing the beach</u>.

What is the meaning of the phrase <u>combing the beach</u> as it is used in this sentence?

A tidying up

B searching the shore

C collecting seashells

D digging holes

3. Determine what each incident from the text reveals about Juan. Write the letter of each character trait next to the incident that reveals it.

Event	Character Trait
Juan's wife gives him a metal detector.	
Juan runs the metal detector over miles of sand.	
Juan bounds out the door with his metal detector.	
Young Juan searched the beach for pirate treasures.	

A Juan is enthusiastic.

B Juan is patient.

C Juan has a vivid imagination.

D Juan is an adult.

Question 3

An author's descriptions can reveal a character's traits. For example, the story says that as young boy Juan loved reader about pirates and spent hours fantasizing about life as a pirate. Think about what those details say about the character Juan.

STOP!

Common Core ELA STANDARDS

RI.8.3
Analyze how a text makes connections among and distinctions between individuals, ideas, or events (e.g., through comparisons, analogies, or categories).

RI.8.4
Determine the meaning of words and phrases as they are used in a text, including figurative, connotative, and technical meanings; analyze the impact of specific word choices on meaning and tone, including analogies or allusions to other texts.

RI.8.6
Determine an author's point of view or purpose in a text and analyze how the author acknowledges and responds to conflicting evidence or viewpoints.

Read this passage and then answer the questions that follow.

What Is Short-Term Stress?

from the Centers for Disease Control and Prevention
http://www.cdc.gov/bam/life/butterflies.html

1   Have you ever started a new school, argued with your best friend, or moved? Do you have to deal with the ups and downs of daily life—like homework or your parents' expectations? Then you already know about stress. In fact, everyone experiences stress. Your body is pre-wired to deal with it— whether it is expected or not. This response is known as the stress response, or fight or flight.

continued ➤

2   The fight or flight response is as old as the hills. In fact, when people used to have to fight off wild animals to survive, fight or flight is what helped them do it. Today, different things cause stress (when was the last time you had to fend off a grizzly bear?), but we still go through fight or flight. It prepares us for quick action—which is why the feeling goes away once whatever was stressing you out passes! It can also happen when something major happens—like if you change schools or have a death in your family.

3   Everyone has weird feelings when they are stressed. Fight or flight can cause things like sweaty palms or a dry mouth when you are nervous, or knots in your stomach after an argument with someone. This is totally normal and means that your body is working exactly like it should. There are lots of signs of stress—common types are physical (butterflies in your stomach), emotional (feeling sad or worried), behavioral (you don't feel like doing things), and mental (you can't concentrate). Most physical signs of stress usually don't last that long and can help you perform better, if you manage them right.

Name_____ Date_____

1. This question has two parts. Answer Part A first. Then answer Part B.

Part A What is the author's view of stress in "What Is Short-Term Stress?"

A It is better that it is short-term than long-term.

B It is a natural and sometimes helpful part of life.

C It is less useful to people now than it was in the past.

D It is something unpleasant all people have to experience.

Question 1
An author's point of view may be directly stated in the text or a reader may need to infer it. In this passage, the author's point of view is stated.

Part B How does this view fit in with the author's purpose in the passage?

A This view helps encourage readers to seek help in dealing with everyday stress.

B This view helps show readers that they should not be upset about feeling stress.

C This view helps prove to readers how similar they are to ancient men and women.

D This view helps convince readers to learn more about the way their bodies function.

continued

Name_____ Date_____

Question 2

To answer this question, think about different meanings of the word *flight*. In this phrase, *flight* is related to the verb *flee*. Knowing the meaning of *flee* should help you answer the question.

2. Read this sentence from "What Is Short-Term Stress?"

> This response is known as the stress response, or <u>fight or flight</u>.

What does <u>fight or flight</u> mean?

A face one's fears or run away from them

B attack one's enemies alone or in a group

C protect oneself from or be attacked by animals

D respond quickly or slowly in a dangerous situation

Question 3

To answer this question, reread the parts of the passage that discuss the similarities and/or differences between early humans and people today.

3. Why does the passage make a connection between early humans and people today?

A to show that the feelings of stress are natural physical responses

B to show that people today have experiences that are very different from those of early humans

C to show that people long ago responded just as quickly in dangerous situations as people do today

D to show that the everyday experiences of early humans are very similar to the experiences of people today

Common Core ELA STANDARDS

RL.8.1
Cite the textual evidence that most strongly supports an analysis of what the text says explicitly as well as inferences drawn from the text.

RL.8.3
Analyze how particular lines of dialogue or incidents in a story or drama propel the action, reveal aspects of a character, or provoke a decision.

RL.8.4
Determine the meaning of words and phrases as they are used in a text, including figurative and connotative meanings; analyze the impact of specific word choices on meaning and tone, including analogies or allusions to other texts.

Read this passage and then answer the questions that follow.

from Chapter 3 of *The Adventures of Tom Sawyer*

by Mark Twain

In this excerpt, Tom Sawyer is painting his Aunt Polly's fence. At first, Tom tries to make the best of it, but quite soon, his enthusiasm for the task quickly fades away.

1   But Tom's energy did not last. He began to think of the fun he had planned for this day, and his sorrows multiplied. Soon the free boys would come tripping along on all sorts of delicious expeditions, and they would make a world of fun of him for having to work—the very thought of it burnt him like fire.

continued ➡

2   He got out his worldly wealth and examined it—bits of toys, marbles, and trash; enough to buy an exchange of work, maybe, but not half enough to buy so much as half an hour of pure freedom. So he returned his straitened means to his pocket, and gave up the idea of trying to buy the boys. At this dark and hopeless moment an inspiration burst upon him! Nothing less than a great, magnificent inspiration.

3   He took up his brush and went tranquilly to work. Ben Rogers hove in sight presently—the very boy, of all boys, whose ridicule he had been dreading. Ben's gait was the hop-skip-and-jump—proof enough that his heart was light and his anticipations high. He was eating an apple, and giving a long, melodious whoop, at intervals, followed by a deep-toned ding-dong-dong, ding-dong-dong, for he was personating a steamboat. As he drew near, he slackened speed, took the middle of the street, leaned far over to starboard and rounded to ponderously and with laborious pomp and circumstance— for he was [im]personating the Big Missouri, and considered himself to be drawing nine feet of water. He was boat and captain and engine-bells combined, so he had to imagine himself standing on his own hurricane-deck giving the orders and executing them.

Name_____ Date_____

1. This question has two parts. Answer Part A first. Then answer Part B.

Part A Read this excerpt from the passage.

> Ben's gait was the hop-skip-and-jump—proof enough that his heart was light and his anticipations high. He was eating an apple, and giving a long, melodious whoop, at intervals, followed by a deep-toned ding-dong-dong, ding-dong-dong, for he was personating a steamboat. As he drew near, he slackened speed, took the middle of the street, leaned far over to starboard and rounded to ponderously and with laborious pomp and circumstance—for he was [im]personating the Big Missouri, and considered himself to be drawing nine feet of water.

What does this description reveal about Ben?

A He is shy.

B He is young.

C He is intelligent.

D He is confident.

Question 1

Think about the descriptive words the author uses to describe Ben and to describe Tom's reaction to Ben. How is Ben walking down the street? What is he doing? What is his mood? Is Tom happy to see him?

Part B What does the passage suggest about Tom's opinion of Ben?

A Tom is terrified of Ben.

B Tom is a little afraid of Ben.

C Tom thinks Ben is ridiculous.

D Tom thinks Ben is different from the other boys.

continued ➡

Name_____ Date_____

Question 2

Use context clues to help you determine the meaning of the phrase *free boys*. For example, the text also says that the boys "would make a world of fun of him for having to work."

2. Read this sentence from the passage.

> Soon the <u>free boys</u> would come tripping along on all sorts of delicious expeditions, and they would make a world of fun of him for having to work—the very thought of it burnt him like fire.

What does the phrase <u>free boys</u> mean as it is used in the sentence above?

A boys who do not have to go to school

B boys who have no chores to do

C boys who have been let out of jail

D boys who do not worry what others think

Question 3

To be correct, there needs to be text evidence to support an inference. Review the answer choices above. Then reread the passage to look for text evidence to support each answer. For example, reread paragraph 2. Is there any evidence in that paragraph that Tom has money to pay his friends? Is there another inference you can make from that paragraph?

3. Which of the following inferences can you make about Tom after reading the passage? Check the box next to each statement you choose.

☐ Tom does not want to be made fun of.

☐ Tom does not like the other boys in his neighborhood.

☐ Tom wants to pay another boy to paint the fence for him.

☐ Tom has money to pay his friends to work.

☐ Tom is trying to find a way out of his situation.

☐ Tom is very tired.

STOP!

Common Core ELA STANDARDS

RI.8.1
Cite the textual evidence that most strongly supports an analysis of what the text says explicitly as well as inferences drawn from the text.

RI.8.2
Determine a central idea of a text and analyze its development over the course of the text, including its relationship to supporting ideas; provide an objective summary of the text.

RI.8.3
Analyze how a text makes connections among and distinctions between individuals, ideas, or events (e.g., through comparisons, analogies, or categories).

RI.8.7
Evaluate the advantages and disadvantages of using different mediums (e.g., print or digital text, video,

multimedia) to present a particular topic or idea.

Read this passage and then answer the questions that follow.

The Storytelling Canyon

1   Each year, over five million people visit the formation known as the Grand Canyon. This geologic wonder, located in Arizona, fascinates scientists and tourists alike with its beauty and its size.

2   Lengthwise, the canyon spans nearly three hundred miles long and as many as eighteen miles wide. In some places it reaches a fear-inducing one mile in depth. The massive cliffs, bold colors, and powerful river below are intriguing enough to make this landmark memorable, but its geological storytelling adds further significance. Erosion caused by the power of moving water formed the Grand Canyon. The Colorado River chiseled the canyon into Earth's crust. This expanse—the canyon—is a unique place where the Earth's floor is literally split open, revealing countless years of the planet's history.

continued ➤

3   Geologists have found almost forty rock layers in the canyon's walls. These strata are a cross-section of approximately two billion years in Earth's history. Fossils, artifacts, and signs of little-known prehistoric eras are inlaid in these rocks. Evidence of volcanic activity streaks the walls as well, which helps scientists identify dates for each rock layer they study.

4   Many of Earth's mysteries hide beneath its surface, buried too deep for scientists to access. For those who specialize in earlier periods of Earth's history, the Grand Canyon is a cherished resource. By studying the different rocks and fossils found in the canyon walls, scientists can access countless clues about the distant past. Time's many layers lie uncovered here, available to teach all they can.

5   Today, the canyon's monumental power continues to draw crowds. People come not only to be astonished and dazzled, but also to see a mile-deep time line of their planet's story, spelled out in jagged stripes and layers of history that may never be fully known.

Name_____ Date_____

1. This question has two parts. Answer Part A first. Then answer Part B.

Part A What is the central idea of "The Storytelling Canyon"?

A The Grand Canyon is a popular tourist destination.

B The Grand Canyon reveals much about Earth's history.

C Many artifacts can be found in the rocks of the Grand Canyon.

D The Colorado River formed the Grand Canyon over millions of years.

Part B How is this central idea developed over the course of the passage?

A Each successive body paragraph gives details from further back in the Earth's history.

B Each successive body paragraph gives a different reason why people visit the canyon.

C First the history of the canyon is described, and then the reasons why people visit the canyon are listed.

D First the formation of the canyon is described, and then the kind of evidence found in the canyon is outlined.

Question 1

Sometimes, as with this passage, the central idea will not be stated in the introduction. When the central idea is not stated, look for an idea that is repeated in the body paragraphs. If an idea is repeated or referred to several times, it is most likely a central idea.

continued →

Name_____ Date_____

Question 2

Look through the passage for information on the Grand Canyon's size and what that size reveals about the canyon.

2. What connection does "The Storytelling Canyon" make between the size of the Grand Canyon and its usefulness to scientists?

A The depth of the canyon allows scientists to study the effects of water erosion on the land.

B The depth of the canyon allows scientists to learn about distant periods in the history of the Earth.

C The length and width of the canyon allow scientists to examine many different types and colors of soil.

D The length and width of the canyon allow scientists to study a large section of the surface of the Earth.

Question 3

One way to locate information in a passage is to skim for *key words*, or important words that the question is asking about. The *key word* for the first inference, for example, is "volcanoes." Skim the text for the word volcano and then reread the text around it.

3. Below are five inferences that can be made from "The Storytelling Canyon." Decide which paragraph each inference can be drawn from. Then write the paragraph number next to the related inference.

Inference	Paragraph	
There were once volcanoes in the area of the Grand Canyon.		
Most of the time, scientists are not able to see fossil evidence deep below the Earth.		
The Grand Canyon is composed of differently colored soils.		
The Earth is billions of years old.		
Water has the strength to wear away rock.		

Name_____ Date_____

4. Would it be better to present this information in a video format or is it better in print? Use examples from the text to support your answer.

_____

_____

_____

_____

_____

_____

Question 4

To answer this question, think about the advantages and disadvantages to seeing a video or movie about a topic.

STOP!

ⓒommon ⓒore ELA
STANDARDS

RL.8.1
Cite the textual evidence that most strongly supports an analysis of what the text says explicitly as well as inferences drawn from the text.

RL.8.3
Analyze how particular lines of dialogue or incidents in a story or drama propel the action, reveal aspects of a character, or provoke a decision.

RL.8.4
Determine the meaning of words and phrases as they are used in a text, including figurative and connotative meanings; analyze the impact of specific word choices on meaning and tone, including analogies or allusions to other texts.

RL.8.6
Analyze how differences in the points of view of the characters and the audience or reader (e.g., created through the use of dramatic irony) create such effects as suspense or humor.

Read this passage and then answer the questions that follow.

Alien Encounter

1   It was a momentous occasion: the first official meeting with an alien race was about to occur, and it was going to happen on Hivelord Styllyk's command ship. Styllyk felt a twinge of nervousness. His people—the inhabitants of the planet Apirax— were so different from these creatures: the aliens had four limbs, two eyes, and no antennae, and their skeletons were completely covered by flesh. They did not use familiar gestures and odors to communicate, like Styllyk's people; instead, they seemed to converse by producing harsh noises from a hole near the top of their bodies.

2   In every previous encounter, Styllyk's people and these creatures had been so afraid of each other that they had not been able to communicate at all. Luckily there had been no mishaps thus far; so when these aliens appeared in a ship near Apirax, Styllyk and his crew were sent out to welcome them. Styllyk was optimistic that they could establish communication.

3   The alien vessel was docking and, in a moment, the hangar bay's hexagonal doors would open, revealing the alien dignitaries. Styllyk wondered if they would show themselves to be peaceful; if these creatures could not find a way to do that, it could mean trouble.

4   Finally, the doors slid open and three aliens walked in, their smelly, fleshy bodies encased in odd, soft coverings. They looked around with their small, ugly eyes. One of them held up a jar filled with a viscous substance, and Styllyk's warrior drones tensed—was that a weapon? The alien opened it up, and the sweet aroma of delicious food filled the chamber. Styllyk fluttered his wings with approval.

5   Captain Buzz of the Earth Space Exploration Fleet turned to his science officer and said, "Good idea bringing honey, Leonard. It will make everything go easier."

Name_____ Date_____

1. This question has two parts. Answer Part A first. Then answer Part B.

Part A Read this sentence from "Alien Encounter."

> The alien vessel was docking and, in a moment, the hangar bay's hexagonal doors would open, revealing the alien <u>dignitaries</u>.

What does the word <u>dignitaries</u> mean?

A important people

B strange creatures

C frightening strangers

D communication experts

Part B Which excerpt from the passage helps you understand the meaning of the word <u>dignitaries</u>?

A They did not use familiar gestures and odors to communicate.

B The first official meeting with an alien race was about to occur.

C Styllyk was optimistic that they could establish communication.

D Styllyk wondered if they would show themselves to be peaceful.

Question 1

Sometimes you can guess the meaning of an unfamiliar word by thinking of a related word whose definition you know. The word *dignitaries* is related to the noun *dignity*. If you know the meaning of *dignity*, you can use this information to help you answer the question.

continued

Name_____ Date_____

Question 2

The point of view of a story is the perspective through which the story is told. It can be a character in the story or an outside narrator who knows the thoughts and feelings of some or all of the characters. To determine the point of view, ask yourself through whose eyes you see the story's events.

2. This question has two parts. Answer Part A first. Then answer Part B.

Part A From whose point of view is "Alien Encounter" told?

A a character in the story who is the leader of an alien race at war with humans

B a character in the story who is a human astronaut meeting aliens for the first time

C an outside narrator who knows the thoughts and feelings of all of the characters in the story

D an outside narrator who knows only the thoughts and feelings of an insect-like alien character

Part B What is the effect of this point of view on the story?

A Humor is created because the reader knows Styllyk does not need to be afraid of Captain Buzz.

B Surprise is created because it is not revealed that the aliens are humans until the end of the story.

C Surprise is created because the reader never finds out the result of the meeting with the aliens.

D Humor is created because Styllyk is more important to his people than Captain Buzz is to Earthlings.

Name_____ Date_____

3. What is the meaning of the word <u>viscous</u> as it is used in the passage?

A golden brown

B thick and sticky

C poisonous

D mean

Question 3

Context clues can help you understand the meaning of this word. In paragraph 4, the substance is revealed to be honey.

4. What can the reader tell about the relationship between the aliens and the inhabitants of Apirax from the story? What does Captain Buzz's dialogue in the final paragraph of "Alien Encounter" reveal about the intentions of the Earth Space Exploration Fleet? Use details from the text to support your answer.

_____

_____

_____

_____

_____

_____

Question 4

To answer this question, underline any details in the text that show the relationship between the aliens and the inhabitants of Apirax. Then make an inference based on the dialogue at the end of the passage. Why do you think Captain Buzz brought honey?

ⓒommon ⓒore ELA
STANDARDS

RI.8.1
Cite the textual evidence that most strongly supports an analysis of what the text says explicitly as well as inferences drawn from the text.

RI.8.2
Determine a central idea of a text and analyze its development over the course of the text, including its relationship to supporting ideas; provide an objective summary of the text.

RI.8.4
Determine the meaning of words and phrases as they are used in a text, including figurative, connotative, and technical meanings; analyze the impact of specific word choices on meaning and tone, including analogies or allusions to other texts.

RI.8.8
Delineate and evaluate the argument and specific claims in a text, assessing whether the reasoning is sound and the evidence is relevant and sufficient; recognize when irrelevant evidence is introduced.

Read this passage and then answer the questions that follow.

Endurance

1   At the turn of the twentieth century, several European countries were locked in a desperate race to be the first to reach the South Pole—an accomplishment that would be a source of national pride. Ernest Shackleton was one of the British explorers competing to reach the South Pole. He was a gifted sailor and disciplined outdoorsman, but history remembers him mostly as a man who triumphed even in his failures.

2   Shackleton was born on February 15, 1874. He enlisted in the merchant navy when he was sixteen. By 1898, he became a master mariner, meaning he was deemed competent to captain his own vessel. His first attempt at reaching the South Pole ultimately failed, yet it sparked his thirst for adventure.

3   Following another futile bid to claim the South Pole for England in 1907, Shackleton saw his dream collapse. In 1911, a Norwegian named Roald Amundsen became the first man to set foot on the South Pole. Undeterred, Shackleton set out on his third and final journey in 1914. Tragedy struck when his ship, the *Endurance*, became trapped in an ice floe off the coast of Antarctica. After ten months of waiting for help, he and his crew abandoned the sinking ship and survived by hunting penguins and seals on floating ice chunks. With supplies dwindling and the hope of survival fading, Shackleton gathered six of his best sailors on a seven-meter boat called the *James Caird*. He left the majority of the crew behind with little more than a promise to return. After crossing 800 miles of choppy seas in sixteen days, Shackleton reached a whaling station on the island of South Georgia. He returned to pick up his remaining crew on August 30, 1916. Despite impossible odds and treacherous terrain, every member of his crew survived.

continued

Name_____ Date_____

Question 1

Sometimes, the context clue for a vocabulary word occurs in the sentence or even the paragraph before the word. For this question, the last sentence of paragraph 2 provides a context clue.

1. Read this sentence from "Endurance."

> Following another <u>futile</u> bid to claim the South Pole for England in 1907, Shackleton saw his dream collapse.

What does the word <u>futile</u> mean as it is used in this passage?

A adventurous

B hopeful

C contentious

D unsuccessful

2. Which of the following details support the inference that the trip Shackleton made to the whaling station on the island of South Georgia was dangerous?

A Became trapped in an ice floe

B After crossing 800 miles of choppy seas

C With supplies dwindling and hopes of survival fading

D He returned to pick up his remaining crew on August 30, 1916.

Question 2

Reread the section of the text that describes Shackleton's trip to South Georgia to check your answer choice.

Name_____ Date_____

3. This question has two parts. Answer Part A first. Then answer Part B.

Part A What is the author's main argument about Shackleton in "Endurance"?

A His talent as a sailor allowed him to find success.

B He was successful at things even when he failed.

C He was unable to complete his most important missions.

D His love of adventure caused him to take on dangerous missions.

Question 3

The strongest expression of an author's argument usually occurs at the end of the passage, where the author sums up his points and makes the final statement of his claims. Reread the end of the passage to help you answer this question.

Part B Is the information presented in the passage sufficient to support this argument?

A Yes, because the passage explains that Shackleton never stopped trying to reach the South Pole.

B Yes, because the passage describes Shackleton's success at the seemingly impossible task to save his stranded crew.

C No, because the passage mostly discusses Shackleton's failure to reach the South Pole.

D No, because the passage describes only one example of Shackleton's saving the men on his crew.

continued

Name_____ Date_____

Question 4

When thinking about the significance of a title, make sure you consider multiple-meaning words. In this case, *Endurance* is the name of Shackleton's ship and it is also a noun that means the ability to survive difficult circumstances.

4. How does the title "Endurance" relate to the ideas in the passage? Use details from the text to support your answer.

_____

_____

_____

_____

_____

_____

_____

Read the passage. Then answer questions 1–10.

from *An Autumn Flood*

by Harriet Myrtle

1 "I am going," said Mary's mamma, on another evening, "to tell you a story about Scotland, and about some children who went there by sea, in a large steamship."

2 Their names were Charlotte, Helen, and Robert, and they went with their papa and mamma to visit their uncle and aunt. They went in August, when the weather is fine, and the days are long. They left home in the evening, for the steamer was to start at ten o'clock at night. There was a great bustle when they came to the place where the ships lie in the River Thames. Many people were getting their trunks and boxes in, and hurrying about. They liked to see all this bustle, and to see their own trunks and boxes put in. Then they stepped on board, across a wide, firm plank, and jumped for joy to find themselves really in the ship, and going to Scotland.

continued ➔

3   It was such a large steamer! They were surprised to see what a length it was. Then they went into a handsome cabin, called the saloon, beautifully lighted, with a great many people in it; and after being there a little while they grew very tired, and their mamma took them to the cabin where they were to sleep. When they saw their beds, they all began to laugh. They looked just like beds made on shelves, one above another. Two were on one side and two on the other, of a kind of closet. But they soon crept in, Charlotte and Helen one above another, and little Robert opposite. The fourth bed was for their nurse, who was going with them. They were all soon asleep. They never knew when the steamer began to go fast down the river towards the sea.

4   In the morning when they awoke, first one and then another heard a constant "thump, thump! bump, bump!" going on. This noise was made by the great engine that turned the paddle-wheels, and moved the ship on. And they felt the ship shaking, and trembling, and rocking, and then they were surprised to hear that they were already out of the River Thames, and had got into the salt sea. They were in a great hurry to be dressed, and when they ran up on the deck they saw the land on one side of them, and numbers of ships all round them, with their white sails shining in the sun, for it was a very fine morning. They tried to count them, but it was very difficult; Charlotte counted a hundred, and Helen a hundred and ten. As to little Robert, he was too delighted to keep steady enough to count, and after trying once or twice, declared that there must be a thousand.

5   Very soon they were called to breakfast in the saloon, and sat by their papa and mamma very happily; but they ran away before they had finished, to see a town called Yarmouth, by which they passed so closely that they could see the houses, and bathing machines [a roofed cart on the beach where people changed into swimwear], and people. All the morning they had plenty to look at. They met other steamers, and fishing-boats, and ships, and saw different places on the coast. But before dinner-time they had lost sight of land, and saw nothing all round them but sea, and did not meet so many ships and boats. Their papa then took them to see the engine, and the great fires down in the engine-room, and made them look at the paddle-wheels, that go foaming round and round. Then came dinner-time, and they were very hungry; and afterwards they amused themselves with running about on the deck and reading story books. Soon after tea they went to bed and fell fast asleep.

Name_____ Date_____

1. This question has two parts. Answer Part A first. Then answer Part B.

Part A Which of the following statements about Charlotte, Helen, and Robert is true?

A Traveling by sea is their favorite thing to do.

B This is their first trip on a large steamship.

C They would rather play than spend time with their parents.

D They have never been to Scotland before.

Part B Which sentence from the passage supports the answer to Part A?

A They were surprised to see what a length it was.

B All the morning they had plenty to look at.

C They never knew when the steamer began to go fast down the river towards the sea.

D They liked to see all this bustle, and to see their own trunks and boxes put in.

continued

Name_____ Date_____

2. This question has two parts. Answer Part A first. Then answer Part B.

Part A Read these sentences from the passage.

> When they saw their beds, they all began to laugh. They looked just like beds made on shelves, one above another.

Why do the children laugh?

A They are relieved that the beds are arranged in this way.

B They have never seen beds like this before.

C They are making fun of the design of their cabin.

D They are nervous about sleeping in such a crowded space.

Part B Which character trait of the children is shown by these lines?

A cheerfulness

B kindness

C snobbishness

D timidity

Name_____ Date_____

3. This question has two parts. Answer Part A first. Then answer Part B.

Part A Read this sentence from the passage.

> Their papa then took them to see the engine, and the great fires down in the engine-room, and made them look at the paddle-wheels, that go <u>foaming</u> round and round.

To what does the <u>foaming</u> refer?

A the sound that the wheels make

B the delicate material from which the wheels are made

C the rough edges of the wheels

D the way the wheels move through the water

Part B What impression is conveyed by the use of the word <u>foaming</u>?

A The wheels are moving the ship powerfully through the sea.

B The children are excited as they watch the wheels.

C Parts of the ship are moving dangerously and recklessly.

D The ocean waves are coming up into the engine room.

continued

Name_____ Date_____

4. This question has two parts. Answer Part A first. Then answer Part B.

Part A What is the **most** exciting part of the trip for the children?

A   time spent with their parents

B   sailing down the river

C   the idea of going to Scotland

D   the many new things to see

Part B Which detail from the passage supports the answer to Part A?

A   The children happily eat breakfast with their parents.

B   The children are overjoyed to be going to Scotland.

C   The children spend the day on deck looking at the coast.

D   The children are surprised that they are no longer on the Thames.

5. Which detail from the text tells the reader that the excerpt from _An Autumn Flood_ takes place in the past?

A   The children are taking a trip to Scotland.

B   The children are traveling by steamship.

C   The children see many ships in the water.

D   The children are leaving at night.

Name_____ Date_____

6. Based on the passage, decide which paragraph each of the following inferences can be drawn from. Then write the paragraph number next to the related inference.

Inference	Paragraph
Robert is the youngest of the children.	
The ship is powered by a flammable material.	
The children's parents sleep in a separate cabin.	
The children want to visit Scotland.	

7. Chose four statements that should be included in a summary of the excerpt from *An Autumn Flood* and number them in the correct order.

— The children are brave when the ship shakes and trembles.

— The family travels to Scotland by steamship.

— The children try to count all the ships they see.

— The children eat breakfast on the boat.

— The children sleep on the boat.

— The children spend the next day exploring the ship and watching the coast.

— They are traveling in August because the weather is nice.

— Three children, their parents, and their nurse are taking a trip to Scotland.

continued

Name_____ Date_____

8. What is the role of the first paragraph in the passage? How is the point of view of this paragraph different from the rest of the passage? Use details from the passage to support your answer.

_____

_____

_____

_____

_____

_____

_____

_____

_____

_____

_____

_____

_____

_____

_____

_____

Name_____ Date_____

9. Read this sentence from the passage.

> Then they stepped on board, across a wide, firm plank, and
> <u>jumped for joy</u> to find themselves really in the ship, and
> going to Scotland.

What impact does the phrase <u>jumped for joy</u> have on the overall meaning of the passage? Why do you think the author uses the phrase <u>jumped for joy</u> instead of saying the children were happy to be on the boat? Use details from the passage to support your answer.

_____

_____

_____

_____

_____

_____

_____

_____

_____

_____

_____

_____

_____

continued

Common Core Reading Warm-Ups & Test Practice Grade 8 • ©2014 Newmark Learning, LLC   Practice Test 1   **67**

Name_____ Date_____

10. What is a theme of the passage? Use details from the passage to support your answer.

_____

_____

_____

_____

_____

_____

_____

_____

_____

_____

_____

_____

_____

_____

_____

_____

_____

STOP!

Read the passage. Then answer questions 1–10.

Australia's Rock Art

1   More than 30,000 years ago, the Aboriginal people of Australia created some of the earliest art on that continent. Many of these creations consisted of paintings or engravings on boulders found in rock shelters and caves.

2   These rock paintings consisted of many different types, including prints and drawings in rock shelters and engravings in limestone caves. One of the most common images found are simple vertical bars; dots and lines were also painted or engraved. Simple stick figures, usually with an outstretched body or even wearing a simple headdress, were also done. Animal drawings were rare, but might depict kangaroos or emus, a type of bird. Hands were commonly painted as well.

continued

3   In order to create their rock art, the Aboriginals had to make their own paint; this was done by collecting red, purple, and yellow pigments from ochre, or clay that is rich in iron. The clay was ground using a stone on a grindstone, then water was added to make the paint. The paints were usually applied by fingers or with simple brushes made of bark or feathers. To create hand stencils, paint was put into the mouth and then sprayed around the person's hand to create an outline. When the hand was removed, a "shadow" image was left. Sometimes, instead of using paint, drawings were made on the surface of the wall with a small lump of ochre. To make engravings, stone tools with blade-like surfaces were used to etch into the stone.

4   People who study the rock art are not quite sure why these early peoples produced the paintings. Some believe that the paintings describe significant events such as a successful hunt or even the first arrival of Europeans to Australia. Others think the paintings were done as part of an important ceremony or ritual. Another theory is that the paintings illustrate the close bond the Aboriginal people had with the land. This idea is very similar to the relationship of Native Americans to their land.

5   Aboriginal rock art has been deemed quite valuable in understanding the early history of Australia. Art historians see rock art as a key to unlocking the mysteries of the early peoples and their culture. For Aboriginal people today, rock art is a reminder of their rich heritage and culture. Unfortunately, because of the delicate nature of the rock shelters and caves, rock art throughout Australia is considered to be an endangered resource. The art is prone to erosion from the elements, and vandalism is also a constant threat to these valuable national treasures. Government officials have undertaken extensive surveys of these cultural landmarks by recording the location, condition, and dimensions of each piece of rock art discovered. Even if the piece is lost, the government will have records so that future generations can learn about Australia's earliest and most noteworthy works of art.

1. Read this sentence from "Australia's Rock Art."

> For Aboriginal people today, rock art is a reminder of their rich <u>heritage</u> and culture.

Which of the following definitions describes the meaning of <u>heritage</u>?

A artwork that contains clues about history

B a group of people that lived long ago

C a book that contains historical records

D something that is passed down through generations

2. This question has two parts. Answer Part A first. Then answer Part B.

Part A According to the passage, why does the government make records of the rock art?

A to protect the art from vandals

B to have a copy in case the art is destroyed

C to remind Aboriginal people of their heritage

D to help understand the early history of Australia

Part B Which sentence from paragraph 5 supports the answer to Part A?

A Aboriginal rock art has been deemed quite valuable in understanding the early history of Australia.

B Art historians see rock art as a key to unlocking the mysteries of the early peoples and their culture.

C The art is prone to erosion from the elements, and vandalism is also a constant threat to these valuable national treasures.

D Even if the piece is lost, the government will have records so that future generations can learn about Australia's earliest and most noteworthy works of art.

continued

Name_____ Date_____

3. This question has two parts. Answer Part A first. Then answer Part B.

Part A Which sentence **best** states the main idea of "Australia's Rock Art"?

A Rock paintings in Australia contain many simple images.

B No one is sure why Aboriginal Australians created art.

C Rock art in Australia is under threat from both humans and the elements.

D Aboriginal rock art is an important national treasure in Australia.

Part B Which sentence from the passage **best** supports the answer to Part A?

A One of the most common images found are simple vertical bars; dots and lines were also painted or engraved.

B Some believe that the paintings describe significant events such as a successful hunt or even the first arrival of Europeans to Australia.

C Government officials have undertaken extensive surveys of these cultural landmarks by recording the location, condition, and dimensions of each piece of rock art discovered.

D For Aboriginal people today, rock art is a reminder of their rich heritage and culture.

Name_____ Date_____

4. What is the author's purpose in paragraph 4?

A to explain that people have different theories about the meaning of the art

B to explain that many people study the art rock art

C to compare the Aboriginals to Native Americans

D to persuade readers that the Aboriginals created the art to describe important events

5. Which sentence **best** states the main idea of paragraph 5?

A Aboriginal rock art is a reminder of the importance and influence of Aboriginal culture in Australia.

B Rock art is delicate and constantly under threat because of its exposure to the elements and vandalism.

C Rock art in Australia is more important than ancient art found in other parts of the world.

D The government of Australia works to record and preserve rock art because of its cultural and historical significance.

continued

Name_____ Date_____

6. Check the box next to each statement that describes a step in the creation of Aboriginal art.

—   Water was added to the clay to make the paint.

—   Ochre is a type of clay rich in iron.

—   The clay was ground on a grindstone with a stone.

—   Paints were applied with fingers or other simple tools.

—   Stone tools were sometimes used to carve into rock.

—   Colored pigments were collected from ochre.

Name_____ Date_____

7. Read the list of details below. Check the box next to each detail that accurately describes a feature of Aboriginal rock art.

❑ simple stick figures

❑ found all over the world

❑ stenciled hand outlines

❑ elaborate drawings of animals

❑ under threat by vandals

❑ consists of paintings and engravings found in rock

❑ created several hundred years ago

❑ stick figures were created using a lump of ochre.

❑ brushes were made from animal hides.

continued ➡

Name_____ Date_____

8. In the conclusion, the author refers to Australia's rock art as "Australia's earliest and most noteworthy works of art." What evidence does the author provide to support the idea that rock art is important to the people of Australia? Use details from the passage to support your answer.

_____

_____

_____

_____

_____

_____

_____

_____

_____

_____

_____

_____

_____

_____

Name_____ Date_____

9. Summarize the theories presented by the author about why the
Aboriginal Australians created art. Use details from the passage to
support your answer.

_____

_____

_____

_____

_____

_____

_____

_____

_____

_____

_____

_____

_____

_____

_____

_____

continued ➡

Name_____ Date_____

Practice Test 2   Common Core Reading Warm-Ups & Test Practice Grade 8 • ©2014 Newmark Learning, LLC

10. Describe how the author organizes information to support the main ideas presented. How does the author's purpose affect the way the information is presented? Include details from the passage to support your answer.

_____

_____

_____

_____

_____

_____

_____

_____

_____

_____

_____

_____

_____

_____

Read the passages. Then answer questions 1–10.

The Blacksmith's Helper

1   Jack bolted down the road to the village square, a carpet of brown and gold crunching beneath his feet along the route. It was late September in Philadelphia, and Jack was finished with schooling for the day. With a little apprehension, he hurried to help at the forge, where his father worked as a blacksmith.

2   Tink, tink—Jack heard the sounds of the metal tool shaping the iron as he approached the shop.

3   "I am here, Father!" Jack said in greeting as he dropped his bookbag at the wooden worktable near the wall. He stood respectfully behind his father, waiting until he was acknowledged. Jack's father turned away from the hearth and stepped back to nod and smile at Jack.

4   "Hello, Jackie, my boy! Are you ready to get to work?" His father handed him a leather apron, which Jack obligingly pulled over his head and tied in the back.

continued

5   "I'm ready," Jack answered hesitantly. Although it would be some years before Jack could be an apprentice to his father, he faithfully came to the forge every day to try to be a good helper. His father was good at finding things for Jack to do, like handing him the proper tools or setting out the pieces of iron.

6   Today Jack's father was tasked with fashioning hammerheads and nails for local customers. Jack watched as his father carefully manipulated the hot iron in the fire using a long set of tongs. He was also working on a wheelbarrow. Strong as an ox, his father moved a heavy piece of iron to the anvil and began to pound away with the hammer.

7   Jack moved to the wooden table where he had his own set of tools. He reached for his hammer, wincing at the memory of the thumb he had struck last week with the metal head of a large mallet. He hesitated, thinking maybe he should sweep the floor instead, but Jack's father glanced at him with a knowing look.

8   "Practice makes perfect!" he said with an encouraging smile.

9   Jack bit his lip and reluctantly picked up the hammer, feeling its smooth wooden handle in his hands. He looked over at his father, who was diligently laboring on the wheelbarrow; Jack pushed his insecurities away and began to work.

10   By day's end, Jack had finished his handiwork and revealed his masterpiece to his father.

11   "Unbelievably clever!" exclaimed Jack's father, overlooking the fact that Jack had nailed an old horseshoe to a wooden block, surrounded by tacks that spelled out his name. "I think you'll make a fine blacksmith one day," he said and smiled proudly at his son.

How Moccasins Were Made

1   There once was a beautiful young woman who lived in a small Lenape village with her family. She was known by everyone near and far to be a kind and benevolent young lady. As it happened, there also lived in the village a young man of notable valor who liked the young woman. In addition to his strength and courage, the young man was known across the breadth of the land for his beautiful flute music.

2   One day the young man traversed to the woman's home. Kneeling outside her *wikiyup*, he played an enchanting melody for her on his flute. On hearing the tune, the young woman was charmed by the beautiful music, and she began to like this young man.

3   The young woman soon stepped outside and spoke to the man, explaining to him how she had to walk out of the wikiyup in her bare feet every morning to grind the corn. She earnestly asked if he might think of a way to protect her feet so they wouldn't get dirty when she walked.

4   The young man was very eager to help the young woman and lessen her troublesome burden. He immediately asked his friends to help him prepare a soft piece of deerskin to put on the ground in front of the woman's wikiyup. In this way, she could walk outside to grind corn and not get her feet dirty.

continued

5   The young woman was exceedingly pleased at what the young man had done for her. She then asked if he could keep her feet from getting dirty when she walked to the creek to fetch water. Instantly, the young man once again roused his friends and asked them to help him retrieve more deer hides.

6   Before long, the man's grandfather saw what was happening and forbade his grandson from taking any more of the village's deerskins, for the people would need them for warm clothing and blankets in the cold winter. The young man explained to his grandfather how much he loved the young woman and desperately wanted to do whatever he could to please her. Seeing the young man's wistful countenance, his grandfather conceded to allow just one more skin. He helped the young man make it soft and cut it in the shape of a foot. He cut another skin similarly and gave them both to the young man to give to the young woman.

7   When the young man placed the moccasins on the woman's feet, she was overjoyed: her feet didn't touch the dirty ground! In time, she married the young man, and they lived together happily in the village; and that's how the first moccasins were made.

Name_____ Date_____

1. This question has two parts. Answer Part A first. Then answer Part B.

Part A Which sentence from "The Blacksmith's Helper" **best** shows how Jack is treated by his father?

A "Are you ready to get to work?"

B "Practice makes perfect!" he said with an encouraging smile.

C Jack's father turned away from the hearth and stepped back to nod and smile at Jack.

D His father was good at finding things for Jack to do, like handing him the proper tools or setting out the pieces of iron.

Part B What is the main result of this treatment?

A Jack creates a work that his father overlooks.

B Jack shows that his skills as a blacksmith are as good as his father's.

C Jack finds the confidence to try his best.

D Jack thinks about the times when he has made mistakes.

continued

Name_____ Date_____

2. This question has two parts. Answer Part A first. Then answer Part B.

Part A Read this sentence from "The Blacksmith's Helper."

> Jack bolted down the road to the village square, a <u>carpet of brown and gold</u> crunching beneath his feet along the route.

Which of the following **best** explains the meaning of the phrase a <u>carpet of brown and gold</u>?

A the leaves that have fallen from the trees

B the dirt of the unpaved road

C the pattern of bricks lining the route

D the dirty ice and snow covering the ground

Part B Which phrase from the passage **best** helps you determine the answer to Part A?

A to the village square

B crunching beneath his feet

C along the route

D late September

Name_____ Date_____

3. This question has two parts. Answer Part A first. Then answer Part B.

Part A Read this sentence from "The Blacksmith's Helper."

> He looked over at his father, who was <u>diligently</u> laboring on the wheelbarrow; Jack pushed his insecurities away and began to work.

What is the meaning of <u>diligently</u> as it is used in the sentence?

A busily

B expertly

C happily

D powerfully

Part B Which detail from the story helps you determine the meaning of <u>diligently</u>?

A Jack's father's wheelbarrow is a masterpiece.

B Jack's father can easily lift heavy things.

C Jack's father works on his tasks all day.

D Jack's father is good at finding jobs for his son.

continued

Name_____ Date_____

4. This question has two parts. Answer Part A first. Then answer Part B.

Part A How does the grandfather help propel the action of "How Moccasins Were Made"?

A   He points out the young man's selfish behavior.

B   He encourages the young man to act according to the rules of the village.

C   He provides a solution to the young man's problem.

D   He helps the young man secretly take the skin from the villagers.

Part B Which sentence from the passage explains why the grandfather acts as he does?

A   Before long, the man's grandfather saw what was happening and forbade his grandson from taking any more of the village's deerskins, for the people would need them for warm clothing and blankets in the cold winter.

B   The young man was very eager to help the young woman and lessen her troublesome burden.

C   The young man explained to his grandfather how much he loved the young woman and desperately wanted to do whatever he could to please her.

D   Seeing the young man's wistful countenance, his grandfather conceded to allow just one more skin.

Name_____ Date_____

5. Which of the following inferences can be made about the Lenape village in the story "How Moccasins Were Made"? Check the box next to each inference that you choose.

❑   The residents of the village walk barefoot.

❑   The village is cold all year round.

❑   The residents of the village share some of their property.

❑   Deerskins are a valuable item in the village.

❑   The grandfather makes all of the rules in the village.

❑   All of the villagers are charmed by the young man's flute playing.

6. Read each element in the chart below. Decide if it can be found in "The Blacksmith's Helper," "How Moccasins Were Made," or both. Put a check mark in the correct box beside each piece of information. If the information is included in both passages, put check marks in both boxes.

Element	The Blacksmith's Helper	How Moccasins Were Made
An older family member who helps by giving emotional support	❑	❑
An older family member who helps by giving practical support	❑	❑
A character who hesitates or doubts and then acts	❑	❑
A character who uses available materials to create something	❑	❑
An explanation that explains the origin of something	❑	❑
Descriptions of a character's inner thoughts	❑	❑

continued

Name_____ Date_____

7. This question has two parts. Answer Part A first. Then answer Part B.

Part A Which of the following is a theme of both "The Blacksmith's Helper" and "How Moccasins Were Made"?

A Creative people can find unique solutions to problems.

B Children should obey their older family members.

C It is important for people to overcome their feelings of self-doubt if they are to succeed in life.

D Sometimes an individual needs help in order to be successful in creating something meaningful.

Part B Which details from the passages support the theme identified in Part A? Check the box next to each detail you choose.

❑ Jack's father works very hard.

❑ Jack gets to work when his father tells him to.

❑ Jack's father encourages him and tells him that "Practice makes perfect."

❑ Jack's father thinks his son's creation is "unbelievably clever."

❑ The beautiful woman in "How Moccasins Were Made" wants something to protect her feet.

❑ The man plays the flute to impress the woman.

❑ The grandfather gives a deer hide to the young man.

❑ The young man creates the first moccasins.

Name_____ Date_____

8. Write a summary of "The Blacksmith's Helper."

_____

_____

_____

_____

_____

_____

9. Over the course of "How Moccasins Were Made," how do the young woman's feelings for the young man develop? Use details from the passage to support your answer.

_____

_____

_____

_____

_____

_____

_____

continued

Name_____ Date_____

10. Compare the use of dialogue in the passages "The Blacksmith's Helper" and "How Moccasins Were Made." Why do you think each story does or does not use dialogue? How does the choice to use or not use dialogue affect the story? Use details from both passages to support your answer.

_____

_____

_____

_____

_____

_____

_____

_____

_____

_____

_____

Read the passages. Then answer questions 1–10.

Constructing a Monument: Stonehenge

1   More than five thousand years ago, the building of one of the most significant structures in England began. Using primitive tools, quite possibly made from deer antlers, a massive circular ditch and bank called a *henge* was constructed. Archaeologists believe that this marked the early creation of one of the most famous prehistoric sites in Great Britain—Stonehenge.

2   The second phase of Stonehenge continued several centuries later when builders hoisted an estimated eighty bluestones into upright positions. It is believed that the stones were then arranged in either a horseshoe or circular formation.

3   A third phase of construction is estimated to have taken place around 2000 B.C.E. This time, sandstone slabs were arranged into a ring that spanned the outside of the bluestones. Some other sandstone slabs were also assembled into three-piece structures that stand in the center of Stonehenge. Only fifty of these stones remain in place today.

continued ▶

4   One of the great puzzles about Stonehenge is how its early builders managed to transport many of the stones, some of which weighed up to four tons. In analyzing the stones, geologists learned that some of the stones, such as the bluestones, were native to an area in Wales, some two hundred miles away from Stonehenge. They believe that the stones were carried to the site by glaciers. The stones were then deposited in the area of Stonehenge. However, archaeologists are dissatisfied with that theory; they are not convinced that glaciers were entirely responsible for moving the stones. Instead, they have offered up their own theories on how the stones came to Stonehenge. One of these suggests that the builders towed the stones by water on rafts. Then the stones were carried over long, grooved planks with the help of oxen.

5   How the stones arrived at Stonehenge is one mystery—but perhaps an even bigger puzzle is what the purpose of the great monument was. Historians all agree that the structure was clearly noteworthy to its builders, but the function of Stonehenge is still unclear. Some believe that the arrangement of stones signifies a large burial site, while others have suggested that it served as a memorial to honor ancient ancestors or perhaps was used as a special ceremonial site. One astronomer even thought that Stonehenge operated as a kind of calendar. More recently, archaeologists have thought that perhaps the bluestones were considered to have special healing powers for those who were ill.

6   Whatever its purpose, Stonehenge is considered one of the most famous and unique historical sites in the world. Thousands of people come to visit every year, and while the true meaning of Stonehenge may never be entirely understood, its vast stone design will undoubtedly continue to puzzle, intrigue, and prove irresistible to people for many more years.

Sister of Stonehenge

1   Located just twenty miles from the giant stone circles of Stonehenge in England stands what some archaeologists refer to as the "wooden twin" of that famed monument—Woodhenge. The site, like its sister site, is what is called a *henge*, which consists of an earthen bank and ditch.

2   Woodhenge was discovered in 1925 by a pilot flying over the area. The pilot noticed a large pattern of rings; fascinated with his discovery, he reported his finding to a local archaeological society, which then began an excavation of the area. In the process, archaeologists discovered a series of egg-shaped outlines that may have held wooden postholes. In addition to the ditch and the bank, the archaeologists also uncovered a more gruesome find: skeletons of a child and a young man in the ditch. Pottery, chalk tools, and flints were also discovered.

3   Slowly, a picture emerged of what the site might have looked like. There was an entrance on the northeast side of the outlines. The postholes were of varying diameters and depths, which suggested that the posts were of different heights.

continued

4   Scientists believe that Woodhenge dates from approximately 2200 to 2300 B.C.E. This is roughly the same time period as the third phase of construction at Stonehenge. They also have inferred that the site originally consisted of six rings of wooden posts surrounding a central point. Archaeologists also discovered at least five standing stones at the site that may have been part of a separate construction phase, like Stonehenge.

5   But are the two sites truly related? While some people have suggested that Woodhenge was a model for Stonehenge, archaeologists disagree. Given the time period of the Woodhenge site, it appears that Stonehenge and Woodhenge were constructed independently of each other.

6   However, the arrangement of the posts and stones suggests more than a passing similarity to Stonehenge. This similarity has led historians and archaeologist to believe that Woodhenge, like Stonehenge, served as a special spiritual area, such as a site for important ceremonies or a burial ground.

7   Today, decorative cement posts mark the spots where the wood posts once stood. And although Woodhenge may not be as well known as its stone neighbor down the road, and its origins are more obscure, it has no shortage of mystery surrounding it. Although many believe that Stonehenge is a unique site, archaeologists are now asking whether there were more sites similar to Stonehenge and Woodhenge. Together, the two sites offer interesting possibilities about the early history and culture of the peoples of England.

Name_____ Date_____

1. This question has two parts. Answer Part A first. Then answer Part B.

Part A Read this sentence from "Constructing a Monument: Stonehenge."

> Thousands of people come to visit every year, and while the true meaning of Stonehenge may never be entirely understood, its vast stone design will undoubtedly continue to puzzle, intrigue, and prove irresistible to people for many more years.

What does the word irresistible mean as it is used in the sentence?

A confusing

B fascinating

C important

D mysterious

Part B Which phrase from the sentence helps you understand the meaning of the word irresistible?

A thousands of people come to visit every year

B the true meaning of Stonehenge

C may never be entirely understood

D vast stone design

continued →

Name_____ Date_____

2. Read this sentence from "Constructing a Monument: Stonehenge."

> One of the great puzzles about Stonehenge is how its early builders managed to transport many of the stones, some of which weighed up to four tons.

What is the role of this sentence in paragraph 4?

A   It introduces information that is hard to explain.

B   It introduces information that might not be accurate.

C   It introduces information for which scientists do not have evidence.

D   It introduces information for which there is only one interpretation.

3. What is a central idea of "Sister of Stonehenge"?

A   Woodhenge, unlike Stonehenge, has been largely rebuilt.

B   Both Woodhenge and Stonehenge were built thousands of years ago.

C   Prehistoric artifacts have been found at both Woodhenge and Stonehenge.

D   Woodhenge, like Stonehenge, is a mysterious site about which we have much to learn.

Name_____ Date_____

4. This question has two parts. Answer Part A first. Then answer Part B.

Part A Which of the following inferences can you make about Woodhenge based on "Sister of Stonehenge"?

A Woodhenge was originally used less than Stonehenge was.

B Woodhenge was redesigned by its builders to look more like Stonehenge.

C Evidence of Woodhenge was hidden for thousands of years.

D Evidence of Woodhenge provides many details about prehistoric England.

Part B Which sentence from the passage supports this inference?

A However, the arrangement of the posts and stones suggests more than a passing similarity to Stonehenge.

B While some people have suggested that Woodhenge was a model for Stonehenge, archaeologists disagree.

C Woodhenge was discovered in 1925 by a pilot flying over the area.

D Archaeologists also discovered at least five standing stones at the site that may have been part of a separate construction phase, like Stonehenge.

continued

Name_____ Date_____

5. This question has two parts. Answer Part A first. Then answer Part B.

Part A Read this sentence from "Sister of Stonehenge."

> In addition to the ditch and the bank, the archaeologists also uncovered a more <u>gruesome</u> find: skeletons of a child and a young man in the ditch.

What does the word <u>gruesome</u> mean as it is used in the sentence?

A fascinating

B frightful

C strange

D serious

Part B What impact does the use of the word <u>gruesome</u> have on the sentence?

A It proves to the reader that the monument was used as a burial site.

B It makes the reader think that the monument is a scary place.

C It helps the reader appreciate how mysterious the site is.

D It convinces the reader that building the site was dangerous work.

Name_____ Date_____

6. This question has two parts. Answer Part A first. Then answer Part B.

Part A Based on the information in both passages, what is one theory that scientists have about both Stonehenge and Woodhenge?

A they were most likely used as a site for burials or important ceremonies

B they were both constructed in stages over hundreds of years

C they were both constructed using materials carried from more than 200 miles away

D they were both used as calendars

Part B According to both passages, how did scientists come to this conclusion?

A written records

B archaeological evidence

C educated guessing

D scientific evaluation

continued

Name_____ Date_____

7. What inferences can be made from the information in "Constructing a Monument: Stonehenge"? Check the box next to each sentence you choose.

☐ Different groups of builders worked on Stonehenge's construction.

☐ Historians hope to find explanatory documents written by Stonehenge's builders.

☐ The circle was an important shape to the people who designed Stonehenge.

☐ The climate of Stonehenge was not always the same as it is now.

☐ Stonehenge was designed to track the monthly movements of the moon.

Name_____ Date_____

8. According to "Sister of Stonehenge," why is Woodhenge called the "wooden twin" of Stonehenge? Use details from the passage to support your answer.

_____

_____

_____

_____

_____

_____

9. According to "Constructing a Monument: Stonehenge," how do scientists identify the different building phases of the monument? Use details from the passage to support your answer.

_____

_____

_____

_____

_____

_____

continued

Name_____ Date_____

10. Do the authors of the passages agree on Stonehenge's uniqueness?
Use details from both passages to support your answer.

_____

_____

_____

_____

_____

_____

_____

_____

_____

_____

_____

_____

from *Heidi* • Warm Up 1

Question & Answer	Standards
1. Identify the text evidence that supports each inference in the chart below. Write the letter in the "Supporting Evidence" column next to the inference it supports.	**RL.8.1**

Inference	Supporting Evidence
Alm is a small town and everyone knows each other.	C
The Alm-Uncle is not a friendly person.	F
The little girl is wearing all of the clothing she owns.	A
Deta wants to reach her destination as soon as possible.	G
Deta resents having to care for the little girl.	D

Question & Answer	Standards
2. Decide which four statements belong in a summary of the excerpt from *Heidi*, and number them in the order they occurred in the passage. A woman asks Deta who the little girl is and where they are going. **[2]** Deta should have continued to care for the little girl. Deta leads a little girl up the mountain and stops in a small village. **[1]** Deta explains that she is taking the little girl to live with her grandfather. **[3]** The mountain is called the Alm. Deta says she will not let the girl keep her from a new opportunity. **[4]** The little girl is hot from being overdressed. It is a bright, sunny day in June.	**RL.8.2**
3 Part A. This question has two parts. Answer Part A first. Then answer Part B. Read this sentence from the excerpt from *Heidi*. The youngster's cheeks were <u>in such a glow</u> that it showed even through her sun-browned skin. What is the meaning of <u>in such a glow</u> as it is used in this sentence? **A red** B shiny C sparkling D sweaty	**RL.8.4**
3 Part B. Which phrase from the text helps you understand the meaning of <u>in such a glow</u>? **A hot and shapeless little person** B leading a little girl by the hand C her feet encased in heavy hob-nailed boots D vigorous maiden of the mountain region	**RL.8.1, RL.8.4**

Weather Patterns • Warm Up 2

Question & Answer	Standards
1 Part A. This question has two parts. Answer Part A first. Then answer Part B. Which inference can be made based on the passage? A Air masses form only over land. **B Understanding jet streams can help people predict local weather.** C Jet streams form only in the United States. D Each of Earth's oceans causes different weather patterns.	**RI.8.1**
1 Part B. Which detail from the text supports the answer to Part A? A A jet stream is a narrow river of very strong winds that forms when two air masses with significant differences in temperature meet. B The larger the temperature difference, the stronger the jet stream. C There is also an event called La Niña in which the equatorial waters of the Pacific Ocean cool. **D Typically, jet stream winds affect the temperatures and precipitation for a few days.**	**RI.8.1**
2. Summarize "Weather Patterns." Choose five statements that belong in a summary of this passage and number them in the order they occur in the passage. Everyone should learn how air masses affect weather. Jet streams affect the weather in a particular area. **[4]** Air masses are carried around the country by jet streams. **[2]** In 2011, it was above 100°F for fifty-two days in a row in Wichita Falls, Texas. Warming and cooling water temperatures in the Pacific Ocean cause some weather patterns. **[5]** Jet streams are strong winds caused by temperature differences between air masses. **[3]** Extreme temperature and precipitation are examples of weather patterns. **[1]** Small temperature differences between air masses lead to longer weather patterns.	**RI.8.2**
3. Read each description and decide whether it applies to El Niño or La Niña. Write the letter in the correct column. <table><tr><th>El Niño</th><th>La Niña</th></tr><tr><td>A</td><td>C</td></tr><tr><td>B</td><td>E</td></tr><tr><td>D</td><td>G</td></tr><tr><td>F</td><td></td></tr><tr><td>H</td><td></td></tr></table>	**RI.8.1, RI.8.4**

The Tryout • Warm Up 3

Question & Answer	Standards
1 Part A. This question has two parts. Answer Part A first. Then answer Part B. Read this sentence from "The Tryout." Kai was aware that earning a spot on the team <u>wasn't going to be a cakewalk</u>, but he was determined to immerse himself in the effort and give it his all. What does the phrase <u>wasn't going to be a cakewalk</u> mean? A would not be fun **B would not be easy** C would not include sweets D would not allow him to walk	**RL.8.4**
1 Part B. Which phrase helps you understand the meaning of <u>wasn't going to be a cakewalk</u>? A planned to ask his father B what Kai lacked in skill **C so he needed all the practice he could get** D hitting was his weakness	**RL.8.1**
2. Read this sentence from "The Tryout." Kai relentlessly threw the baseball at a net that was designed to return the ball to him. What does this sentence tell readers about Kai? A Kai is able to throw the baseball at high speeds. B Kai does not understand the rules of baseball. **C Kai is willing to spend a lot of time working toward his goal.** D Kai does not have enough energy to find his ball after he throws it.	**RL.8.3**
3 Part A. This question has two parts. Answer Part A first. Then answer Part B. What is the central idea of this passage? **A It takes hard work and dedication to try out for a team.** B Only people with experience will make the team. C Eating a healthy diet is the most important part of getting in shape. D Participating in sports is more important than academic success.	**RL.8.2**
3 Part B. Which detail from the text best supports the answer to Part A? A All athletes get in shape by drinking smoothies. B His parents had always encouraged him to succeed at academics in school. C The other players would have experience, speed, agility, and strength. **D He was determined to immerse himself in the effort and give it his all.**	**RL.8.2**

The Bone Wars • Warm Up 4

Question & Answer	Standards
1 Part A. This question has two parts. Answer Part A first. Then answer Part B. Which statement is a central idea of "The Bone Wars"? A Competition leads to handsome rewards. B Scientific rivals will stop at nothing to win. **C The rivalry of the scientists had both positive and negative results.** D Colorado holds the most important dinosaur fossils found.	**RI.8.2**
1 Part B. Which of the following details from the text support your answer to Part B? Check the box next to each statement you choose. ❑ **Their work had left both men almost penniless.** ❑ The contest between the two climaxed in 1877, with the discovery of fossils at two separate sites in Colorado. ❑ It would appear that Marsh won the Bone Wars, with his discovery of some eighty new dinosaur fossils ❑ By 1892, the Bone Wars had come to an end. ❑ **It is believed that over 142 new species were discovered as a result of their work.** ❑ Although the relationship between Marsh and Cope was forever tainted, the findings by both men galvanized the American public's growing interest in dinosaurs.	**RI.8.2**
2. Read this sentence from "The Bone Wars." For both men, there were no measures too extreme or too outrageous in the race to become the reigning dinosaur hunter. How does this sentence help develop a key concept of the text? A It summarizes the creative ideas the men had as they hunted fossils. **B It introduces the idea that the men did many awful things in an effort to win.** C It provides a detailed description of specific behaviors the men engaged in. D It supports the idea that winning is more important than gaining scientific knowledge.	**RI.8.5**
3. Determine which comparisons the author provides to show how Cope and Marsh are similar. Check the box next to each statement you choose. ❑ **Both spied on the other's dig sites.** ❑ Both saved their reputations by discovering so many new species. ❑ **Both despised the other.** ❑ Both discovered the *Stegosaurus* and *Brontosaurus*. ❑ **Both wanted the title of "Best Dinosaur Hunter."** ❑ **Both had their workers destroy fossils so the other could not find them.** ❑ Both fought over gold. ❑ **Both lost all of their money by the end of the Bone Wars.** ❑ **Both bribed workers.**	**RI.8.3**

An Unexpected Treasure • Warm Up 5

Question & Answer	Standards
1 Part A. This question has two parts. Answer Part A first. Then answer Part B. Which of the following inferences can you make from the passage? **A** **Juan found a license plate.** B Juan wishes he was a pirate. C Juan is frustrated with the hunt along the beach. D Juan learns how to work the metal detector at the end of the day.	**RL.8.1**
1 Part B. Which detail from the text supports the answer to Part A? A Juan's stomach was rumbling, and he thought it was probably time to call it a day. B Juan dug and dug, his mind whirring with possibilities. **C** **His eyes grew wide, he held his breath, and he scraped his hand across a thin metal placard that read: 093-BFX.** D With fingers trembling, Juan ran the disk of his metal detector back over the spot, straining his ears to hear the digital alarm sound out again.	**RL.8.1**
2. Read this sentence from "An Unexpected Treasure." He flinched at the noise; he hadn't heard so much as a blip in all his hours <u>combing the beach</u>. What is the meaning of the phrase <u>combing the beach</u> as it is used in this sentence? A tidying up **B** **searching the shore** C collecting seashells D digging holes	**RL.8.4**
3. Determine what each incident from the text reveals about Juan. Write the letter of each character trait next to the incident that reveals it. <table><tr><th>Event</th><th>Character Trait</th></tr><tr><td>Juan's wife gives him a metal detector</td><td>F</td></tr><tr><td>Juan ran the metal detector over miles of sand</td><td>B</td></tr><tr><td>Juan bounds out the door with his metal detector</td><td>A</td></tr><tr><td>Young Juan searched the beach for pirate treasures</td><td>D</td></tr></table>	**RL.8.3**

What Is Short-Term Stress? • Warm Up 6

Question & Answer	Standards
1 Part A. This question has two parts. Answer Part A first. Then answer Part B. What is the author's view of stress in "What Is Short-Term Stress?" A It is better that it is short-term than long-term. **B It is a natural and sometimes helpful part of life.** C It is less useful to people now than it was in the past. D It is something unpleasant all people have to experience.	**RI.8.6**
1 Part B. How does this view fit in with the author's purpose in the passage? A This view helps encourage readers to seek help in dealing with everyday stress. **B This view helps show readers that they should not be upset about feeling stress.** C This view helps prove to readers how similar they are to ancient men and women. D This view helps convince readers to learn more about the way their bodies function.	**RI.8.6**
2. Read this sentence from "What Is Short-Term Stress?" This response is known as the stress response, or <u>fight or flight</u>. What does <u>fight or flight</u> mean? **A face one's fears or run away from them** B attack one's enemies alone or in a group C protect oneself from or be attacked by animals D respond quickly or slowly in a dangerous situation	**RI.8.4**
3. Why does the passage make a connection between early humans and people today? **A to show that the feelings of stress are natural physical responses** B to show that people today have experiences that are very different from those of early humans C to show that people long ago responded just as quickly in dangerous situations as people do today D to show that the everyday experiences of early humans are very similar to the experiences of people today	**RI.8.3**

from Chapter 3 of *The Adventures of Tom Sawyer* • Warm Up 7

Question & Answer	Standards
1 Part A. This question has two parts. Answer Part A first. Then answer Part B. Read this excerpt from the passage. Ben's gait was the hop-skip-and-jump–proof enough that his heart was light and his anticipations high. He was eating an apple, and giving a long, melodious whoop, at intervals, followed by a deep-toned ding-dong-dong, ding-dong-dong, for he was personating a steamboat. As he drew near, he slackened speed, took the middle of the street, leaned far over to starboard and rounded to ponderously and with laborious pomp and circumstance–for he was [im]personating the Big Missouri, and considered himself to be drawing nine feet of water. What does this description reveal about Ben? A He is shy. B He is young. C He is intelligent. **D He is confident.**	RL.8.3
1 Part B. What does the passage suggest about Tom's opinion of Ben? A Tom is terrified of Ben. **B Tom is a little afraid of Ben.** C Tom thinks Ben is ridiculous. D Tom thinks Ben is different from the other boys.	RL.8.3
2. Read this sentence from the passage. Soon the <u>free boys</u> would come tripping along on all sorts of delicious expeditions, and they would make a world of fun of him for having to work–the very thought of it burnt him like fire. What does the phrase <u>free boys</u> mean as it is used in the sentence above? A boys who do not have to go to school **B boys who have no chores to do** C boys who have been let out of jail D boys who do not worry what others think	RL.8.4
3. Which of the following inferences can you make about Tom after reading the passage? Check the box next to each statement you choose. ❏ **Tom does not want to be made fun of.** ❏ Tom does not like the other boys in his neighborhood. ❏ **Tom wants to pay another boy to paint the fence for him.** ❏ Tom has money to pay his friends to work. ❏ **Tom is trying to find a way out of his situation.** ❏ Tom is very tired.	RL.8.1

The Storytelling Canyon • Warm Up 8

Question & Answer	Standards
1 Part A. This question has two parts. Answer Part A first. Then answer Part B. What is the central idea of "The Storytelling Canyon"? A The Grand Canyon is a popular tourist destination. **B The Grand Canyon reveals much about Earth's history.** C Many artifacts can be found in the rocks of the Grand Canyon. D The Colorado River formed the Grand Canyon over millions of years.	RI.8.2
1 Part B. How is this central idea developed over the course of the passage? A Each successive body paragraph gives details from further back in the Earth's history. B Each successive body paragraph gives a different reason why people visit the canyon. C First the history of the canyon is described, and then the reasons why people visit the canyon are listed. **D First the formation of the canyon is described, and then the kind of evidence found in the canyon is outlined.**	RI.8.2
2. What connection does "The Storytelling Canyon" make between the size of the Grand Canyon and its usefulness to scientists? A The depth of the canyon allows scientists to study the effects of water erosion on the land. B The depth of the canyon allows scientists to learn about distant periods in the history of the Earth. **C The length and width of the canyon allow scientists to examine many different types and colors of soil.** D The length and width of the canyon allow scientists to study a large section of the surface of the Earth.	RI.8.3
3. Below are five inferences that can be made from "The Storytelling Canyon." Decide which paragraph each inference can be drawn from. Then write the paragraph number next to the related inference.	RI.8.1

Inference	Paragraph
There were once volcanoes in the area of the Grand Canyon.	3
Most of the time, scientists are not able to see fossil evidence deep below the Earth.	4
The Grand Canyon is composed of differently colored soils.	2
The Earth is billions of years old.	3
Water has the strength to wear away rock.	2

	Standards
4. Would it be better to present this information in a video format or is it better in print? Use examples from the text to support your answer. **Sample answer:** It would be better to present this information in a visual format because the viewer would be better able to understand the size of the canyon by seeing a video of it. In addition, the viewer would be able to see the different layers of rock in the canyon.	RI.8.7

Alien Encounter • Warm Up 9

Question & Answer	Standards
1 Part A. This question has two parts. Answer Part A first. Then answer Part B. Read this sentence from "Alien Encounter." The alien vessel was docking and, in a moment, the hangar bay's hexagonal doors would open, revealing the alien <u>dignitaries</u>. What does the word <u>dignitaries</u> mean? **A important people** B strange creatures C frightening strangers D communication experts	RL.8.4
1 Part B. Which excerpt from the passage helps you understand the meaning of the word <u>dignitaries</u>? A They did not use familiar gestures and odors to communicate. **B The first official meeting with an alien race was about to occur.** C Styllyk was optimistic that they could establish communication. D Styllyk wondered if they would show themselves to be peaceful.	RL.8.1, RL.8.4
2 Part A. This question has two parts. Answer Part A first. Then answer Part B. From whose point of view is "Alien Encounter" told? A a character in the story who is the leader of an alien race at war with humans B a character in the story who is a human astronaut meeting aliens for the first time C an outside narrator who knows the thoughts and feelings of all of the characters in the story **D an outside narrator who knows only the thoughts and feelings of an insect-like alien character**	RL.8.6
2 Part B. What is the effect of this point of view on the story? A Humor is created because the reader knows Styllyk does not need to be afraid of Captain Buzz. **B Surprise is created because it is not revealed that the aliens are humans until the end of the story.** C Surprise is created because the reader never finds out the result of the meeting with the aliens. D Humor is created because Styllyk is more important to his people than Captain Buzz is to Earthlings.	RL.8.6
3. What is the meaning of the word <u>viscous</u> as it is used in the passage? A golden brown **B thick and sticky** C poisonous D mean	RL.8.4

Question & Answer	Standards
4. What can the reader tell about the relationship between the aliens and the inhabitants of Apirax from the story? What does Captain Buzz's dialogue in the final paragraph of "Alien Encounter" reveal about the intentions of the Earth Space Exploration Fleet? Use details from the text to support your answer.	**RL.8.3**
Sample answer: The aliens and the inhabitants of Apirax have been afraid of each other and unable to communicate. Styllyk describes how the aliens seemed to converse through harsh noises, and when the aliens first arrive on the ship, the warrior drones think the honey might be a weapon. Captain Buzz's dialogue shows that the fleet knew that Styllyk was bee-like and would enjoy the special gift of honey. This reveals that Captain Buzz wants to establish a good relationship with the alien race.	

Endurance • Warm Up 10

Question & Answer	Standards
1. Read this sentence from "Endurance." Following another <u>futile</u> bid to claim the South Pole for England in 1907, Shackleton saw his dream collapse. What does the word <u>futile</u> mean as it is used in this passage? A adventurous B hopeful C contentious **D unsuccessful**	**RI.8.4**
2. Which of the following details support the inference that the trip Shackleton made to the whaling station on the island of South Georgia was dangerous? A Became trapped in an ice floe **B After crossing 800 miles of choppy seas** C With supplies dwindling and hopes of survival fading D He returned to pick up his remaining crew on August 30, 1916.	**RI.8.2**
3 Part A. This question has two parts. Answer Part A first. Then answer Part B. What is the author's main argument about Shackleton in "Endurance"? A His talent as a sailor allowed him to find success. **B He was successful at things even when he failed.** C He was unable to complete his most important missions. D His love of adventure caused him to take on dangerous missions.	**RI.8.8**
3 Part B. Is the information presented in the passage sufficient to support this argument? A Yes, because the passage explains that Shackleton never stopped trying to reach the South Pole. **B Yes, because the passage describes Shackleton's success at the seemingly impossible task to save his stranded crew.** C No, because the passage mostly discusses Shackleton's failure to reach the South Pole. D No, because the passage describes only one example of Shackleton's saving the men on his crew.	**RI.8.8**
4. How does the title "Endurance" relate to the ideas in the passage? Use details from the text to support your answer. **Sample answer:** The title "Endurance" relates to both the name of Shackleton's ship and the quality he needed to survive his trip to Antarctica. First, Shackleton had to endure ten months trapped off the coast of Antarctica. Then, Shackleton and a group of six men had to take a dangerous trip across 800 miles of sea to get help for his crew.	**RI.8.1, RI.8.2**

from *An Autumn Flood* • Practice Test 1

Question & Answer	Standards
1 Part A. This question has two parts. Answer Part A first. Then answer Part B. Which of the following statements about Charlotte, Helen, and Robert is true? A Traveling by sea is their favorite thing to do. **B This is their first trip on a large steamship.** C They would rather play than spend time with their parents. D They have never been to Scotland before.	**RL.8.2**
1 Part B. Which sentence from the passage supports the answer to Part A? **A They were surprised to see what a length it was.** B All the morning they had plenty to look at. C They never knew when the steamer began to go fast down the river towards the sea. D They liked to see all this bustle, and to see their own trunks and boxes put in.	**RL.8.1**
2 Part A. This question has two parts. Answer Part A first. Then answer Part B. Read these sentences from the passage. When they saw their beds, they all began to laugh. They looked just like beds made on shelves, one above another. Why do the children laugh? A They are relieved that the beds are arranged in this way. **B They have never seen beds like this before.** C They are making fun of the design of their cabin. D They are nervous about sleeping in such a crowded space.	**RL.8.3**
2 Part B. Which character trait of the children is shown by these lines? **A cheerfulness** B kindness C snobbishness D timidity	**RL.8.3**
3 Part A. This question has two parts. Answer Part A first. Then answer Part B. Read this sentence from the passage. Their papa then took them to see the engine, and the great fires down in the engine-room, and made them look at the paddle-wheels, that go <u>foaming</u> round and round. To what does the <u>foaming</u> refer? A the sound that the wheels make B the delicate material from which the wheels are made C the rough edges of the wheels **D the way the wheels move through the water**	**RL.8.4**

Question & Answer	Standards
3 Part B. What impression is conveyed by the use of the word <u>foaming</u>? **A The wheels are moving the ship powerfully through the sea.** B The children are excited as they watch the wheels. C Parts of the ship are moving dangerously and recklessly. D The ocean waves are coming up into the engine room.	**RL.8.4**
4 Part A. This question has two parts. Answer Part A first. Then answer Part B. What is the **most** exciting part of the trip for the children? A time spent with their parents B sailing down the river C the idea of going to Scotland **D the many new things to see**	**RL.8.2**
4 Part B. Which detail from the passage supports the answer to Part A? A The children happily eat breakfast with their parents. B The children are overjoyed to be going to Scotland. **C The children spend the day on deck looking at the coast.** D The children are surprised that they are no longer on the Thames.	**RL.8.1**
5. Which detail from the text tells the reader that the excerpt from *An Autumn Flood* takes place in the past? A The children are taking a trip to Scotland. **B The children are traveling by steamship.** C The children see many ships in the water. D The children are leaving at night.	**RL.8.2**
6. Based on the passage, decide which paragraph each of the following inferences can be drawn from. Then write the paragraph number next to the related inference.	**RL.8.1**

Inference	Paragraph
Robert is the youngest of the children.	4
The ship is powered by a flammable material.	5
The children's parents sleep in a separate cabin.	3
The children want to visit Scotland.	2

	Standards
7. Chose four statements that should be included in a summary of the excerpt from *An Autumn Flood* and number them in the correct order. The children are brave when the ship shakes and trembles. The family travels to Scotland by steamship. **[2]** The children try to count all the ships they see. The children eat breakfast on the boat. The children sleep on the boat. **[3]** The children spend the next day exploring the ship and watching the coast. **[4]** They are traveling in August because the weather is nice. Three children, their parents, and their nurse are taking a trip to Scotland. **[1]**	**RL.8.2**

Question & Answer	Standards
8. What is the role of the first paragraph in the passage? How is the point of view of this paragraph different from the rest of the passage? Use details from the passage to support your answer.	**RL.8.3, RL.8.6**
Sample answer: The first paragraph of the passage is not part of the story of the steamship voyage and it has a different point of view. It is told from the point of view of the person listening to the story. The rest of the passage switches to the point of view of Charlotte, Helen, and Robert. Everything that happens on the ship is told through their eyes. The reader only learns about what they experience and how they feel. For example, when the engines turn on in paragraph 4 the reader learns about it through the children's eyes: "they felt the ship shaking . . . and then they were surprised to hear that they were already out of the River Thames."	
9. Read this sentence from the passage.	**RL.8.4**
Then they stepped on board, across a wide, firm plank, and <u>jumped for joy</u> to find themselves really in the ship, and going to Scotland.	
What impact does the phrase <u>jumped for joy</u> have on the overall meaning of the passage? Why do you think the author uses the phrase <u>jumped for joy</u> instead saying the children were happy to be on the boat? Use details from the passage to support your answer.	
Sample answer: The phrase "jumped for joy" shows an overwhelming happiness. The phrase highlights how excited the children are to be going on the trip and characterizes them as young and easily pleased. This characterization is continued throughout the rest of the passage, where they are described as continually "running" and "laugh[ing]." These behaviors fit in with the initial characterization of them as "jumping for joy."	
10. What is a theme of the passage? Use details from the passage to support your answer.	**RL.8.2**
Sample answer: A theme of the passage is the excitement of young children when doing something new and pleasurable. Throughout the passage, the children meet each new experience with happiness and energy. They "jump for joy" when they board the ship. They are described three times as running: "up on the deck," "away" from breakfast, and "about on the deck." All this running conveys the children's energy and unflagging excitement. They are eager to see everything they can. They are excited "to see all the bustle" when they board the boat. They leave breakfast to "see a town called Yarmouth." They enjoy counting all the ships they see and they go down to see the engines. It would be difficult to imagine an adult or even a teenager behaving in the same way.	

Australia's Rock Art • Practice Test 2

Question & Answer	Standards
1. Read this sentence from "Australia's Rock Art." For Aboriginal people today, rock art is a reminder of their rich <u>heritage</u> and culture. Which of the following definitions describes the meaning of <u>heritage</u>? A artwork that contains clues about history B a group of people that lived long ago C a book that contains historical records **D something that is passed down through generations**	**RI.8.4**
2 Part A. This question has two parts. Answer Part A first. Then answer Part B. According to the passage, why does the government make records of the rock art? A to protect the art from vandals **B to have a copy in case the art is destroyed** C to remind Aboriginal people of their heritage D to help understand the early history of Australia	**RI.8.1**
2 Part B. Which sentence from paragraph 5 supports the answer to Part A? A Aboriginal rock art has been deemed quite valuable in understanding the early history of Australia. B Art historians see rock art as a key to unlocking the mysteries of the early peoples and their culture. C The art is prone to erosion from the elements, and vandalism is also a constant threat to these valuable national treasures. **D Even if the piece is lost, the government will have records so that future generations can learn about Australia's earliest and most noteworthy works of art.**	**RI.8.1**
3 Part A. This question has two parts. Answer Part A first. Then answer Part B. Which sentence **best** states the main idea of "Australia's Rock Art"? A Rock paintings in Australia contain many simple images. B No one is sure why Aboriginal Australians created art. C Rock art in Australia is under threat from both humans and the elements. **D Aboriginal rock art is an important national treasure in Australia.**	**RI.8.1**
3 Part B. Which sentence from the passage **best** supports the answer to Part A? A One of the most common images found are simple vertical bars; dots and lines were also painted or engraved. B Some believe that the paintings describe significant events such as a successful hunt or even the first arrival of Europeans to Australia. C Government officials have undertaken extensive surveys of these cultural landmarks by recording the location, condition, and dimensions of each piece of rock art discovered. **D For Aboriginal people today, rock art is a reminder of their rich heritage and culture.**	**RI.8.1**

Question & Answer	Standards
4. What is the author's purpose in paragraph 4? A to explain that people have different theories about the meaning of the art **B to explain that many people study the rock art** C to compare the Aboriginals to Native Americans D to persuade readers that the Aboriginals created the art to describe important events	**RI.8.6**
5. Which sentence **best** states the main idea of paragraph 5? A Aboriginal rock art is a reminder of the importance and influence of Aboriginal culture in Australia. B Rock art is delicate and constantly under threat because of its exposure to the elements and vandalism. C Rock art in Australia is more important than ancient art found in other parts of the world. **D The government of Australia works to record and preserve rock art because of its cultural and historical significance.**	**RI.8.5**
6. Check the box next to each statement that describes a step in the creation of Aboriginal art. ❏ **Water was added to the clay to make the paint.** ❏ Ochre is a type of clay rich in iron. ❏ **The clay was ground on a grindstone with a stone.** ❏ **Paints were applied with fingers or other simple tools.** ❏ Stone tools were sometimes used to carve into rock. ❏ **Colored pigments were collected from ochre.**	**RI.8.2**
7. Read the list of details below. Check the box next to each detail that accurately describes a feature of Aboriginal rock art. ❏ **simple stick figures** ❏ found all over the world ❏ **stenciled hand outlines** ❏ elaborate drawings of animals ❏ **under threat by vandals** ❏ **consists of paintings and engravings found in rock** ❏ created several hundred years ago ❏ Stick figures were created using a lump of ochre. ❏ Brushes were made from animal hides	**RI.8.2**

Question & Answer	Standards
8. In conclusion, the author refers to Australia's rock art as "Australia's earliest and most noteworthy works of art." What evidence does the author provide to support the idea that rock art is important to the people of Australia? Use details from the passage to support your answer. **Sample answer:** Rock art is important to the people of Australia for several reasons. The rock art was created by Aboriginal Australians. The art is a reminder of the cultural contributions of the Aboriginal people to Australia. Historians believe that the art holds answers to questions about the lives of early Australians.	**RI.8.8**
9. Summarize the theories presented by the author about why the Aboriginal Australians created art. Use details from the passage to support your answer. **Sample answer:** According to the passage, some people believe that the rock art represents important events that occurred in the lives of the artists, for example, a successful hunt or the first Europeans visiting Australia. Others think the art was created as part of a ceremony or ritual. A final theory is that the art represented a bond with the land.	**RI.8.2**
10. Describe how the author organizes information to support the main ideas presented. How does the author's purpose affect the way the information is presented? Include details from the passage to support your answer. **Sample answer:** The author's purpose in writing this passage is to inform the reader about rock art in Australia. The author supports the main ideas in the passage by presenting information in paragraphs, each of which contains a main idea that is supported by relevant details. The author includes information about where rock art is found, how it was created, why it is important to the people of Australia, and how the government is preserving the art. Because the author's purpose is to inform the reader, the details included are mostly facts. Only a few speculations are included.	**RI.8.3**

The Blacksmith's Helper • How Moccasins Were Made • Practice Test 3

Question & Answer	Standards
1 Part A. This question has two parts. Answer Part A first. Then answer Part B. Which sentence from "The Blacksmith's Helper" **best** shows how Jack is treated by his father? A "Are you ready to get to work?" **B "Practice makes perfect!" he said with an encouraging smile.** C Jack's father turned away from the hearth and stepped back to nod and smile at Jack. D His father was good at finding things for Jack to do, like handing him the proper tools or setting out the pieces of iron	**RL.8.1**
1 Part B. What is the main result of this treatment? A Jack creates a work that his father overlooks. B Jack shows that his skills as a blacksmith are as good as his father's. **C Jack finds the confidence to try his best.** D Jack thinks about the times when he has made mistakes	**RL.8.3**
2 Part A. This question has two parts. Answer Part A first. Then answer Part B. Read this sentence from "The Blacksmith's Helper." Jack bolted down the road to the village square, <u>a carpet of brown and gold</u> crunching beneath his feet along the route. Which of the following **best** explains the meaning of the phrase a <u>carpet of brown and gold</u>? **A the leaves that have fallen from the trees** B the dirt of the unpaved road C the pattern of bricks lining the route D the dirty ice and snow covering the ground	**RL.8.4**
2 Part B. Which phrase from the passage best helps you determine the answer to Part A? A to the village square **B crunching beneath his feet** C along the route D late September	**RL.8.1**

Question & Answer	Standards
3 Part A. This question has two parts. Answer Part A first. Then answer Part B. Read this sentence from "The Blacksmith's Helper." He looked over at his father, who was <u>diligently</u> laboring on the wheelbarrow; Jack pushed his insecurities away and began to work. What is the meaning of <u>diligently</u> as it is used in the sentence? **A busily** B expertly C happily D powerfully	**RL.8.4**
3 Part B. Which detail from the story helps you determine the meaning of <u>diligently</u>? A Jack's father's wheelbarrow is a masterpiece. B Jack's father can easily lift heavy things. **C Jack's father works on his tasks all day.** D Jack's father is good at finding jobs for his son.	**RL.8.4**
4 Part A. This question has two parts. Answer Part A first. Then answer Part B. How does the grandfather help propel the action of "How Moccasins Were Made"? A He points out the young man's selfish behavior. B He encourages the young man to act according to the rules of the village. **C He provides a solution to the young man's problem.** D He helps the young man secretly take the skin from the villagers.	**RL.8.3**
4 Part B. Which sentence from the passage explains why the grandfather acts as he does? A Before long, the man's grandfather saw what was happening and forbade his grandson from taking any more of the village's deerskins, for the people would need them for warm clothing and blankets in the cold winter. B The young man was very eager to help the young woman and lessen her troublesome burden. C The young man explained to his grandfather how much he loved the young woman and desperately wanted to do whatever he could to please her. **D Seeing the young man's wistful countenance, his grandfather conceded to allow just one more skin.**	**RL.8.1**
5. Which of the following inferences can be made about the Lenape village in the story "How Moccasins Were Made"? Check the box next to each inference that you choose. ❏ **The residents of the village walk barefoot.** ❏ The village is cold all year round. ❏ **The residents of the village share some of their property.** ❏ **Deerskins are a valuable item in the village.** ❏ The grandfather makes all of the rules in the village. ❏ All of the villagers are charmed by the young man's flute playing.	**RL.8.1**

Question & Answer			Standards
6. Read each element in the chart below. Decide if it can be found in "The Blacksmith's Helper," "How Moccasins Were Made," or both. Put a check mark in the correct box beside each piece of information. If the information is included in both passages, put check marks in both boxes.			**RL.8.2, RL.8.6**

Element	The Blacksmith's Helper	How Moccasins Were Made
An older family member who helps by giving emotional support	✔	✔
An older family member who helps by giving practical support		✔
A character who hesitates or doubts and then acts	✔	
A character who uses available materials to create something	✔	✔
An explanation that explains the origin of something		✔
Descriptions of a character's inner thoughts	✔	

Question & Answer	Standards
7 Part A. This question has two parts. Answer Part A first. Then answer Part B. Which of the following is a theme of both "The Blacksmith's Helper" and "How Moccasins Were Made"? A Creative people can find unique solutions to problems. B Children should obey their older family members. C It is important for people to overcome their feelings of self-doubt if they are to succeed in life. **D Sometimes an individual needs help in order to be successful in creating something meaningful.**	**RL.8.2**
7 Part B. Which details from the passages support the theme identified in Part A? Check the box next to each detail you choose. ❏ Jack's father works very hard. ❏ Jack gets to work when his father tells him to. ❏ **Jack's father encourages him and tells him that "Practice makes perfect."** ❏ Jack's father thinks his son's creation is "unbelievably clever." ❏ The beautiful woman in "How Moccasins Were Made" wants something to protect her feet. ❏ The man plays the flute to impress the woman. ❏ **The grandfather gives a deer hide to the young man.** ❏ The young man creates the first moccasins.	**RL.8.1, RL.8.2**

Question & Answer	Standards
8. Write a summary of "The Blacksmith's Helper."	**RL.8.2**
Sample answer: Jack runs to the village square to the forge where his father works as a blacksmith. He arrives at the forge and is greeted by his father. Jack puts on a leather apron as he prepares to help, and he watches his father work. Jack moves to the table with his own tools and has doubts about handling them. Encouraged by his father, Jack finds the confidence to make something with the tools and materials at hand. His father praises Jack's finished creation.	
9. Over the course of "How Moccasins Were Made," how do the young woman's feelings for the young man develop? Use details from the passage to support your answer.	**RL.8.1, RL.8.2**
Sample answer: Over the course of "How Moccasins Were Made," the young woman's feelings for the young man change from liking to loving him. When she first hears the music he plays for her, she begins "to like" him. Later, after the young man places the deerskins on the ground for her, she is "exceedingly pleased." When he gives her the moccasins, she is even happier—she is "overjoyed." The young man's help causes her to fall in love with him, and she eventually marries him and lives with him "happily."	
10. Compare the use of dialogue in the passages "The Blacksmith's Helper" and "How Moccasins Were Made." Why do you think each story does or does not use dialogue? How does the choice to use or not use dialogue affect the story? Use details from both passages to support your answer.	**RL.8.1, RL.8.3, RL.8.5**
Sample answer: Dialogue is used in "The Blacksmith's Helper" but not in "How Moccasins Were Made." "The Blacksmith's Helper" is a short story, and it uses dialogue to reveal things about the characters. Jack's dialogue ("I am here, Father!" and "I'm ready") reveals that Jack is eager and ready to help his father. His father's dialogue ("Hello, Jackie, my boy!", "Unbelievably clever!", and "I think you'll make a fine blacksmith one day") reveals that he loves Jack and wants to encourage him in any way he can. "How Moccasins Were Made" is a myth and does not include any dialogue. Instead, what the characters say is indirectly reported. The story says that the young man "immediately asked his friends to help him," but it does not give his exact words. The young woman "asked if he could keep her feet from getting dirty," and again the story does not give her exact words. Since this is a myth and not a short story, the telling of the story, not the development of the characters, is what is important. The indirect dialogue is used not to reveal character but to move the story along. Stating the dialogue indirectly also gives the reader the feeling that the myth tells about something that happened a long time ago.	

Constructing a Monument: Stonehenge • Sister of Stonehenge • Practice Test 4

Question & Answer	Standards
1 Part A. This question has two parts. Answer Part A first. Then answer Part B. Read this sentence from "Constructing a Monument: Stonehenge." Thousands of people come to visit every year, and while the true meaning of Stonehenge may never be entirely understood, its vast stone design will undoubtedly continue to puzzle, intrigue, and prove <u>irresistible</u> to people for many more years. What does the word <u>irresistible</u> mean as it is used in the sentence? A confusing **B fascinating** C important D mysterious	**RI.8.4**
1 Part B. Which phrase from the sentence helps you understand the meaning of the word <u>irresistible</u>? **A thousands of people come to visit every year** B the true meaning of Stonehenge C may never be entirely understood D vast stone design	**RI.8.1**
2. Read this sentence from "Constructing a Monument: Stonehenge." One of the great puzzles about Stonehenge is how its early builders managed to transport many of the stones, some of which weighed up to four tons. What is the role of this sentence in paragraph 4? **A It introduces information that is hard to explain.** B It introduces information that might not be accurate. C It introduces information for which scientists do not have evidence. D It introduces information for which there is only one interpretation.	**RI.8.5**
3. What is a central idea of "Sister of Stonehenge"? A Woodhenge, unlike Stonehenge, has been largely rebuilt. B Both Woodhenge and Stonehenge were built thousands of years ago. C Prehistoric artifacts have been found at both Woodhenge and Stonehenge. **D Woodhenge, like Stonehenge, is a mysterious site about which we have much to learn.**	**RI.8.2**
4 Part A. This question has two parts. Answer Part A first. Then answer Part B. Which of the following inferences can you make about Woodhenge based on "Sister of Stonehenge"? A Woodhenge was originally used less than Stonehenge was. B Woodhenge was redesigned by its builders to look more like Stonehenge. **C Evidence of Woodhenge was hidden for thousands of years.** D Evidence of Woodhenge provides many details about prehistoric England.	**RI.8.3**

Question & Answer	Standards
4 Part B. Which sentence from the passage supports this inference? A However, the arrangement of the posts and stones suggests more than a passing similarity to Stonehenge. B While some people have suggested that Woodhenge was a model for Stonehenge, archaeologists disagree. **C Woodhenge was discovered in 1925 by a pilot flying over the area.** D Archaeologists also discovered at least five standing stones at the site that may have been part of a separate construction phase, like Stonehenge.	RI.8.1
5 Part A. This question has two parts. Answer Part A first. Then answer Part B. Read this sentence from "Sister of Stonehenge." In addition to the ditch and the bank, the archaeologists also uncovered a more <u>gruesome</u> find: skeletons of a child and a young man in the ditch. What does the word <u>gruesome</u> mean as it is used in the sentence? A fascinating **B frightful** C strange D serious	RI.8.4
5 Part B. What impact does the use of the word <u>gruesome</u> have on the sentence? A It proves to the reader that the monument was used as a burial site. B It makes the reader think that the monument is a scary place. **C It helps the reader appreciate how mysterious the site is.** D It convinces the reader that building the site was dangerous work.	RI.8.4
6 Part A. This question has two parts. Answer Part A first. Then answer Part B. Based on the information in both passages, what is one theory that scientists have about both Stonehenge and Woodhenge? **A they were most likely used as a site for burials or important ceremonies** B they were both constructed in stages over hundreds of years C they were both constructed using materials carried from more than 200 miles away D they were both used as calendars	RI.8.2, RI.8.3
6 Part B. According to both passages, how did scientists come to this conclusion? **A written records** B archaeological evidence C educated guessing D scientific evaluation	RI.8.2

Question & Answer	Standards
7. What inferences can be made from the information in "Constructing a Monument: Stonehenge"? Check the box next to each sentence you choose. ❏ **Different groups of builders worked on Stonehenge's construction.** ❏ Historians hope to find explanatory documents written by Stonehenge's builders. ❏ **The circle was an important shape to the people who designed Stonehenge.** ❏ **The climate of Stonehenge was not always the same as it is now.** ❏ Stonehenge was designed to track the monthly movements of the moon.	**RI.8.1, RI.8.2**
8. According to "Sister of Stonehenge," why is Woodhenge called the "wooden twin" of Stonehenge? Use details from the passage to support your answer. **Sample answer**: Woodhenge is called the "wooden twin of Stonehenge" for two reasons. First, Woodhenge is Stonehenge's "twin" because both monuments contain a "henge" surrounded by a circular construction. It is the "wooden twin" because the circular construction in Woodhenge was made of "wooden posts," while the circular construction in Stonehenge was made of stones.	**RI.8.1, RI.8.2**
9. According to "Constructing a Monument: Stonehenge," how do scientists identify the different building phases of the monument? Use details from the passage to support your answer. **Sample answer:** Scientists identify the different building phases of Stonehenge by the materials used and the construction done. In the first phase, primitive tools, possibly "deer antlers," were used to make a "massive circular ditch." In the second phase, "80 bluestones" were arranged in a "horseshoe or circular formation." In the third phase, "sandstone slabs" were arranged in a "ring that spanned the outside of the bluestones."	**RI.8.1, RI.8.2**
10. Do the authors of the passages agree on Stonehenge's uniqueness? Use details from both passages to support your answer. **Sample answer:** The authors of the passages do not agree on Stonehenge's uniqueness. "Constructing a Monument: Stonehenge" argues that Stonehenge is unique. The passage states that "Stonehenge is considered one of the most famous and unique historical sites in the world." It also states that Stonehenge is "one of the most significant structures in England." This statement implies that there are no other sites similar to Stonehenge; if there were, it would no longer be one of the "most significant" sites but just one of many. "Sister of Stonehenge," on the other hand, states that Stonehenge is not unique and that there is at least one other site, Woodhenge, that is similar to it. The passage calls Woodhenge the "wooden twin" of Stonehenge and compares the structures and dates of construction of the two monuments. It also states that archaeologists today are not like "those who believe that Stonehenge is a unique site." They believe there may be "more sites similar to Stonehenge and Woodhenge."	**RI.8.1, RI.8.6, RI.8.9**